VINCENZO VENEZIA

attachment theory
in relationships

Useful Tools to Increase Stability and Build Happy and Lasting Bonds. A Journey from Childhood to Adulthood

TABLE OF CONTENTS

INTRODUCTION

John Bowlby and Mary Ainsworth are jointly credited with the invention of attachment theory. John Bowlby is credited with developing the main elements of the theory. He drew ideas and inspiration from other domains, including ethology, cybernetics, information processing, developmental psychology, and psychoanalysts. As a result, he drastically altered our understanding of the bond between a child and his or her mother and how that bond may be ruptured by events such as abandonment, deprivation, and loss. Mary Ainsworth's innovative research methodology made it feasible to undertake empirical tests on some of John Bowlby's ideas. It also contributed to the theory's growth and is responsible for some of the new directions it is presently taking. Ainsworth is credited with conceptualizing the hypothesis that infants need an attachment figure to feel comfortable enough to go out into the greater world.

The creation of the concept of maternal sensitivity to newborn signals and the significance of this sensitivity in establishing infant-mother attachment patterns was another contribution she made. This sensitivity contributes to the development of attachment patterns between babies and mothers. The development of the concepts now used to drive attachment theory may be traced back over a prolonged and complicated period. Freud and other psychoanalytical thinkers influenced both Bowlby and Ainsworth's work, although Freud had a bigger direct influence on Bowlby's work than on Ainsworth's. Bowlby and Ainsworth started their careers independently of one another and worked independently for most of their early careers. In this chapter, I trace the conceptual origins of ideas that play significant roles in the development of attachment theory, including attachment security and secure attachment. I will then go on to describe the second era of theory development and consolidation.

Finally, I will analyze new avenues into which the theory is now expanding and speculate on its prospects. I will also discuss some novel channels via which the idea spreads. If we follow the development from its conclusion backward, the chain of events seems to be continuous, and we get the impression that our knowledge is entirely adequate or even exhaustive. However, if we begin with the premises that can be drawn from the analysis and follow them to their conclusion, we no longer get the feeling that there was an inescapable sequence of events that could not have been decided in any other manner. This is because we base our arguments on deducible premises from the analysis. In my narrative of the development of attachment theory, since I detail how each new thought and methodological development functioned as a stepping stone for the next, the process of constructing a theory seems more planned and ordered than it is. There is no question that this was true to some extent, yet it is possible that those involved did not perceive it this way when this research was occurring.

In 1948, Bowlby recruited James Robertson to assist him in observing sick and institutionalized children who had been removed from their parents. Ainsworth was among the children that were observed. During World War II, Robertson worked as a boilerman at Anna Freud's Hampstead residential nursery for homeless children, which provided him with an exceptional education in the trade of naturalistic observation. During the war, he also served as a conscientious objector. Anna Freud mandated that all staff members, regardless of expertise or experience, record observations of the children's behavior on index cards. These statements served as a springboard for weekly group talks held inside the institution.

The comprehensive training in child observation that the Hampstead residential nursery made available to Robertson is regarded as Anna Freud's most important and lasting individual contribution to the growth and refining of attachment theory. After two years of gathering data on hospitalized children for Bowlby's study projects, Robertson complained that he could not continue as an uninvolved research worker but felt driven to do something for the children he had been observing. He then filmed the immensely touching film *A Two-Year-Old Goes to Hospital* on a low budget and without artificial lighting using a hand-held cinecamera. This film, along with Spitz's (1947) *Grief: A Peril in Infancy*, was crucial in increasing the level of care offered to hospitalized infants across the Western hemisphere, despite early hostility from the established medical establishment.

Mary Boston and Dina Rosenbluth were already working in Bowlby's research section when Mary Ainsworth joined the team at the close of 1950. During that time, James Robertson was the only other employee. Christoph Heinicke and Tony Ambrose joined the group in 1961. Both of these scholars were engaged in social behavior development. Later, Rudolph Schaffer joined the group. Mary Ainsworth, responsible for evaluating James Robertson's data, was profoundly impressed by his records of children's behavior. As a result, she concluded that if she ever decided to conduct her own inquiry, she would model her observation tactics after Robertson's naturalistic approach.

Bowlby was commissioned by Ronald Hargreaves of the World Health Organization (WHO) to publish a study on the mental health of homeless children in postwar Europe due to his prior publications concerning the family experiences of affectionless children. During the study's development, Bowlby consulted with several European and American practitioners and academics interested in the effects of maternal separation and deprivation on newborns. It took six months to complete the research, released by the World Health Organization in 1951 under the title "Maternal Care and Mental Health." It was translated into fourteen languages, and the English paperback version sold 400,000 copies. *Child Care and the Growth of Love* is the revised and updated version of the 1965 Penguin Books publication. Mary Ainsworth wrote the review chapters included in this edition.

The study revealed some astonishing new insights. Bowlby used the prevailing psychoanalytic language of the time (love object, libidinal connections, ego, and super-ego), but his beliefs were nothing short of heretical at the time they were created. He probably attempted to emulate Spitz when he used embryology to describe the mother's involvement in her child's growth. According to him, for development to proceed healthily, the tissues must be exposed to the action of the proper organizer at critical times. Similarly, it seems vital for mental growth that the undifferentiated psyche is exposed to the influence of the psychic organizer – the mother – during certain crucial phases of development. This allows for the normal growth of the intellect. Bowlby asserts that during the early years, when a child is developing the ability to self-regulate, the mother is the child's ego and super-ego; this seems to refute the notion that the super-ego derives from the resolution of the Oedipus complex.

It should not come as a surprise to hear that these functions either do not operate or function with the greatest degree of imprecision imaginable throughout infancy and early childhood. Consequently, the infant is completely reliant on his mother to carry out these tasks on his behalf at this essential growth stage. She gives him a sense of his location in space and time, supplies him with his surroundings, and helps him to satisfy certain desires while suppressing others. She represents his ego and super-ego for him. As time passes, he trains himself to do these activities independently, and as he does so, the parent delegates more and more responsibilities to him. This gradual, nuanced, and ongoing process starts when he learns to walk and feed himself, and continues until he becomes an adult. The development of a child's ego and super-ego are closely linked to his fundamental interpersonal connections. This material is more consistent with the Vygotskian hypothesis than with the Freudian view. In addition, despite Bowlby's disagreements with Kleinian therapy, I detect Kleinian ideas in his discussions of children's violent fantasies upon returning to their parents after a period of prolonged separation, and the intense depression that humans experience as a result of hating the person they love and need the most.

Bowlby concluded, based on the available empirical evidence at the time, that for a child to develop a healthy mind, they should experience a warm, intimate, and continuous relationship with his mother (or primary caregiver) in which both find satisfaction and enjoyment. Bowlby was also interested in social networks' role in developing healthy mother-child relationships. In the same way that a child's well-being is wholly reliant on parental care and attention, adults, especially women, are often compelled to rely on the financial support of the greater society. This is particularly true in nations where women are less likely to retain steady jobs.

If culture appreciates and respects its children, it must also cherish and respect the people who rear them. The efforts by Bowlby, in a way typical of the age during which the WHO study was prepared, placed great emphasis on the mother's role. He observes that men may benefit their children while they are babies, but they often play a subordinate position to the mother after that. While carrying out their duties as primary caregivers, wives' primary responsibility is to provide emotional support to their husbands. A theoretical explanation of this phenomenon was necessitated by the notion that for children to grow emotionally to their full potential, loving adults must offer them continuous and in-depth interaction. Bowlby was dissatisfied with the prevalent psychoanalytic theory at the time, which held that maternal love arises from oral sensual fulfilment. He also rejected social learning theory's assertion that dependence depends on secondary reinforcement. Bowlby felt that love for the mother stems from a mixture of these two elements. However, he was quite critical of both stances (a concept derived from psychoanalytic ideas). Like Spitz (1946) and Erikson (1950), Bowlby became enamored with the notion of critical stages in embryonic development. A friend introduced him to the English translation of Konrad Lorenz's (1935) work on imprinting while he was seeking equivalent phenomena at the behavioral level. At the time, he was searching for comparable behavioral events. Imprinting is the process through which an organism gains the capacity to respond to its environment.

Bowlby then started scouring the discipline of ethology for fresh insights. Lorenz's article on imprinting in geese and other precocial birds piqued his interest because it demonstrated that the creation of social bonds was not always inexorably linked to food intake. In addition, he gave ethological approaches for studying animals in their natural environments high importance. Because this concept fits so well with the procedures that Robertson had previously devised at the Tavistock research center, he also advocated for its use.

Bowlby's ability to recruit great persons who were willing and able to aid him in learning was a significant skill that served him well throughout his career. For example, he conversed with Robert Hinde to increase his knowledge of ethology.

Bowlby was then able to comprehend the ethological concepts that allowed him to generate new ways of thinking about infant-mother bonding due to Hinde's "generous and severe instruction."

Similarly, Hinde's fascinating study on individual variability in separation and reunion behaviors of group-living rhesus mother-infant dyads was inspired by his interactions with Bowlby and his colleagues. Booth's Hinde and Spencer study was completed in 1967. The many empirical studies on the effects of separation that Bowlby's research team published around the same period show no indication of Bowlby's new way of thinking, which is quite surprising. His colleagues at the time did not feel that ethology influenced the attachment between a mother and child. Even Mary Ainsworth, who was very committed to the study of ethology, had reservations about the course that Bowlby's thinking had started to take. It had become crystal clear to her that a child adores his mother because she meets all of his needs.

Despite this, a 1956 study authored by Bowlby, Ainsworth, Boston, and Rosenbluth is notable because it foreshadows Ainsworth's future work on attachment patterns. Ainsworth's contribution to the paper was a classification system for three fundamental relationship patterns in school-age children who had been reunited with their parents after extended stays in a sanatorium: those with strong positive feelings toward their mothers, those with markedly ambivalent relationships, and the third group with no expressive, indifferent, or hostile relationships with their mother.

PART 1 – AN INTRODUCTION TO ATTACHMENT THEORY

Chapter 1

WHAT IS ATTACHMENT THEORY?

1.1. What is Attachment Theory?

The main premise of attachment theory is that primary caregivers who are readily available and responsive to the infant's requirements help the infant establish a sense of security. The child learns that their caregiver is trustworthy and secure, which provides a solid foundation for the child to explore the world. Attachment theory is one of the most influential and well-known theories in psychology.

1.1.1. The Origins of Attachment Theory

John Bowlby noticed children struggled to form close relationships with other children while working with delinquent and maladjusted youths in the 1930s. Bowlby looked at the family histories of these children and found that many had experienced disruptions in their lives from an early age. He concluded that healthy development depends on the strong emotional bonds between parents and children at an early age. Bowlby looked at a variety of perspectives in order to create his ideas. These included psychodynamic theories; cognitive, developmental psychology; and ethics (the science of human behavior and animal behavior within the contexts of evolution). He determined that children's attachment behavior evolved to ensure that the child could remain safe and secure with their caregivers. Infants use gestures, sounds, and other signals to draw attention to adults and keep in touch with them.

1.2. John Bowlby's Attachment Theory

The theory of etiology greatly inspired Bowlby. Lorenz had proven that attachment was inborn (in the earliest stages of development in ducks) and, therefore, could be a source of survival. Likewise, in the development of humankind, it was the infants who remained near their mothers that generally survived to have their own children. Bowlby believed that mothers and infants had developed an instinctual need to remain connected. He thought that attachment behavior (such as seeking proximity) was instinctual and that the terror that can arise from encountering strangers can be considered a vital survival technique that is inherent to us.

1.2.1. Main Ideas of Bowlby's Theory

The main postulates of Bowlby's theory are given below:

- **A child is born with an inborn need to connect to**

a single attachment image (i.e., monotropy).

His theory suggests that attachment is crucial to the development of a child. The attachment behavior of infants with their mothers was developed through natural selection. The result is that babies have been genetically programmed to develop innate behavior to ensure that attachment occurs. Other attachments may be a part of a hierarchy underneath this. Such attachments may include a child's siblings or father, for instance. But Bowlby claims that the mother's bond is distinct from other relationships.

In essence, he suggested that a breakdown of the maternal bond could cause serious negative consequences. Bowlby's monotropy theory was the basis for formulating his mother's deprivation theory. The child's behavior serves as a prompt for contact from or proximity to the person caring for them. Smiles, crying, and even a fluttering of the feet are all instances of these behavior signals. Instinctively the caregivers respond to the child's actions and develop different ways to respond and keep the child engaged.

- **The child needs to be under constant supervision from the mother for first two years of their life.**

If attachment to the primary caregiver is damaged or destroyed in the two crucial first years, the child may suffer devastating consequences. For example, should it be acceptable for the primary caregiver to take their child to a daycare facility so they can start working?

- **There may be a number of long-term effects of deprivation from mother.**

Bowlby's theory on deprivation from motherhood suggests that an ongoing interruption in the relationship between the primary caregiver could cause lasting interpersonal, social, and cognitive difficulties for the child. These may include:

- Misconduct

- Lower intelligence

- Aggressiveness

- Despondency

- Apathy

- Inability to express love or care for other people.

These individuals may also be driven by impulse and may not think about what their choices mean.

- **A brief separation from an attachment character can trigger stress.**

Working alongside James Robertson (1952), John Bowlby observed that children were under stress when they were away from their mothers. The researchers identified three different stages of stress:

- Protest: An infant may cry, scream and protest in anger after the parent has left. They try to hold onto the parent to prevent them from going away.

- Sadness: The child's screaming ends, and they appear more relaxed, even though they are still agitated. The child cannot accept other people's attempts to soothe them and often withdraws and is disinterested in all activities.

- Separation: If the separation process is not removed, the child might start interacting with other children and begin to interact with others. They will be angry with the caregiver upon returning to their home.

- **The link between the child's relationships with his/her primary caregiver plays a role in the development of their internal models that determine how they function.**

The working model of our brains is known as a cognitive framework. This includes mental representations that help us understand ourselves, the universe, and the world around us. People's interactions with others are influenced by their experiences and expectations from their internal model, which affects and aids in evaluating their interactions with others (Bretherton and Munholland, 1999). In the words of Bowlby (1969), the primary caregiver is an example for future relationships through an internal model of how to work.

The three major characteristics that make up the inner working model of the self are:

- The model of the world as reliable,

- A model of the self that is important; and

- An image of the self that is effective in working with other people.

This mental model of the brain will guide future emotional and social behavior in the same way the child's internal functioning model determines their response to the world around them.

1.2.2. Adult Romantic Relationships

Bowlby was primarily concerned with the relationship between infant and caregiver. He believed attachment was the basis of the human experience, from "cradle to grave." After the 1980s, researchers began to look into the possibility of attachment in adulthood. Hazan (1987) and Shaver (1997) first explored Bowlby's ideas in the context of romantic relationships. They believe that adult romantic partners share an emotional bond partly because they have the same motivational system, the behavioral attachment system. In addition, they found similar responses between adult partners, and an infant and their caregiver. For example:

- Both feel secure when the other person is close by and responsive.

- Both engage in intimate, close bodily contact.

- Both can feel insecure if the other is unavailable.

- Both share their discoveries.

- Both show mutual interest in one another and play with each other's facial features.

- Both may engage in "baby talk."

Based on these parallels, Hazan and Shaver argued that adult romantic relationships, just like infant-caregiver relations, are attachments, and that romantic love is a property of both the attachment behavioral and motivational systems that lead to caregiving and sexuality.

1.2.3. Three Implications of Adult Attachment Theory

Research on close relationships has greatly influenced the idea of romantic relationships as attachment relationships. This concept has at least three implications. Firstly, if adult romantic relationships are a form of attachment, we should observe similar individual differences between adult relationships and infant-caregiver relationships, as discussed above.

We might expect adults to feel secure in their relationships. They should be able and willing to depend on their partners. But insecure adults may be anxious and/or resistant. They may worry that others do not love them enough and can become frustrated or angry if they do not get what their heart desires. Some people may avoid certain situations. Others may not be as concerned about having intimate relationships, and might prefer not to be dependent on others.

Secondly, if adult romantic relationships are attachment relationships, then the way adult relationships "work" should be the same for infant-caregiver relationships. The same factors enable exploration in children. For example, being able to communicate with your caregiver should be a key factor in adult exploration. Being able to communicate with your partner is important.

Thirdly, whether an adult feels secure in adult relationships or not could partly be a result of their experiences with their primary caregivers. Bowlby believed mental representations and working models (i.e., expectations, beliefs, or scripts for thinking/behaving) are the results of our past experiences. Because of their previous experiences, a secure child will trust that others will be there for him or her. A child sets these expectations, and they will seek out relationships that meet them. Bowlby says this process should encourage continuity in attachment patterns throughout life. However, an individual's attachment pattern can change if their relational experiences are inconsistent with their expectations. If we consider adult relationships to be attachment relationships, then it is possible for children who are secure as children to grow up to be secure with their romantic relationships. Similarly, people who feel secure in their adult relationships with their parents are more likely to form secure relationships with new partners. These three implications are briefly discussed in the following sections, based on contemporary and early research on adult attachment.

1.2.4 Are Adult Romantic Relationships the Same as Infant-Caregiver Relations?

Research shows that adult-caregiver relationships are similar to infant-caregiver relations. However, there are notable exceptions. Researchers found that adults who separated from their partners at an airport showed attachment-related behavior and caregiving. Naturalistic research also confirmed this. Separating couples showed more attachment behavior than non-separating couples. However, high-functioning adults showed significantly less attachment behavior than seen in the infant-caregiver relationship. Below are some parallels between adult romantic relationships and infant-caregiver relationships:

- **Partner selection**

Cross-cultural research suggests that mothers prefer a secure attachment pattern in infancy. Of course, no comparable study asks infants whether they prefer an attachment that promotes security. According to Zeifman and Hazan (1997), adults looking for long-term relationships find responsive caregiving qualities such as warmth, attentiveness, and sensitivity to be the most attractive in potential partners. However, not all adults match with secure partners, although they are attractive for their secure qualities. Evidence suggests that people are attracted to partners who share their attachment beliefs.

- **Haven behavior and secure base**

People with secure attachment were well-adjusted in infancy. They are resilient and get along well with their peers. Research on adult attachment has shown similar patterns. In general, secure adults are happier in their relationships than insecure adults. They have greater trust, commitment, interdependence, and longevity in their relationships.

Additionally, they are more likely to use romantic partners as a safe base from which to explore the world. Research on adult attachment has focused on discovering the psychological and behavioral mechanisms that support security and secure base behavior in adults. Insecure people often attribute their partner's behavior to conflict situations and subsequent relationships. This can exacerbate their insecurity rather than relieve it.

• Avoidant Attachment and Defense Mechanisms

Attachment theory says that children have different strategies for managing attachment-related anxiety. For example, insecure children might approach their parents with ambivalence, resistance, or hostility after a divorce or reunion. Some children withdraw from their parents to reduce attachment-related emotions and behaviors. Many questions have been raised about infant attachment and whether children who withdraw from their parents (avoidant) are less distressed, or if their defensive behavior masks their vulnerability. Researchers have found that children who avoid their parents are more distressed than those who do not. However, they also show a calm, defensive attitude.

Recent research on adult attachment has revealed fascinating complexities about the relationship between defense and avoidance. Some avoidant adults are called fearful-avoidant adults, and others are described as dismissing adults. They are capable of using adaptive defensive strategies. Fraley and Shaver (1997) found that adults who were asked to talk about losing their partner were as emotionally distressed as the rest of the population (as measured by skin conductance), even when they exhibited dismissive tendencies. However, these individuals could effectively suppress their feelings and thoughts when instructed. They could, in other words, deactivate some of their physiological arousals and reduce the attention they paid to attachment-related thoughts. People who were fearful of their emotions were less successful at suppressing them.

1.2.5. Is It Possible To Maintain Attachment Patterns From Infancy Through Adulthood?

Adult attachment theory's most controversial and provocative conclusion is that a person's attachment style can be affected by how they interact with their parents. Although it is not hard to imagine that early attachment experiences could influence romantic attachment style, there has been controversy about how these two attachment styles might overlap. When examining the question of stability, there are at least two things to consider: (a) How similar is the security that people experience with different people (e.g., mothers, fathers, or romantic partners)? (b) How stable is security throughout a relationship?

This first issue is related to the fact that there appears to be a slight overlap in how secure people feel about their mothers and romantic partners. Fraley collected self-report measures about one's current attachment style and shared them with a significant parent figure and a romantic partner. The correlations between these two types of attachment relationships ranged from .20 to 0.50 (small to moderate). Concerning the second issue, it appears that the stability of one's attachment to one's parents equals a correlation of .25 and.39 (Fraley 2002). Only one longitudinal study has examined the relationship between security at the age of one and the security of the same person 20 years later in their adult relationships. The unpublished study found a correlation between these variables of .17 (Steele Waters Crowell & Treboux 1998).

Retrospective studies also examined the relationship between attachment styles and early attachment experiences. For example, Hazan and Shaver (1987) found that people who feel secure in romantic relationships were more likely than not to have had a happy childhood. Some writers claim that attachment theory's main proposition is that the attachment system, which was originally designed for the ecology in infancy, still influences behavior, thought, and feelings in adulthood (Fraley & Shaver, 2000).

Attachment theorists suggest that stability in attachment style is not the norm. However, the basic mechanisms can predict long-term continuity or discontinuity, depending on how they are conceptualized. Fraley (2002) presented two models of continuity that were derived using attachment theory. They make different predictions about long-term continuity, even though they are based on the same theoretical principles. Both models assume that attachment representations of individuals are affected by early experiences with caregivers. These experiences influence the quality and quantity of subsequent attachment experiences. One model assumes that the existing representations are constantly updated and revised to reflect new experiences, so they are eventually "overwritten."

According to mathematical analyses, this model predicts that individual differences will remain stable over the long term. The second model is identical to the first but assumes that representational models created in the first year are not overwritten and will continue to impact relational behavior throughout life. This model showed that stability over the long term could reach a non-zero limit value. The important point is that attachment theory principles can be used to create developmental models that make dramatically different predictions about long term stability for individual differences.

1.2.6. Attachment Behavior is Instinctual

Attachment is an emotional bonding and mental compatibility between two persons. Bowlby advised that attachment will help keep children close to their mother, thus increasing the odds of survival of the child. He considered attachment to be the result of the evolutionary processes. Theories suggest that attachment is an acquired behavior. However, Bowlby and others proposed that children have an instinctual drive to create bonds with their caregivers.

In the past, children who were close to a loved one were more likely to have safety and comfort and were more likely to make it to adulthood. Through natural selection, a motivating system to regulate attachment developed. What factors determine the success of attachment? Behaviorists claim that food was the factor that triggered the attachment behavior, but Bowlby and colleagues demonstrated that responsiveness and solemnity were the main factors.

1.3. The Stages of Attachment

Researchers Rudolph Schaffer and Peggy Emerson investigated the degree of attachment bonds infants form during a study carried out over a lengthy time period. Sixty infants were surveyed every four weeks throughout the first few months of their lives, and once after 18 months. Based on the findings, Schaffer and Emerson described the four phases that define attachment:

- ***Pre-Attachment Stage***

From birth to three months, infants do not exhibit any specific affection for a particular caregiver. Instead, the baby's behaviors, such as crying or screaming, naturally grab their caregiver's attention. Likewise, the child's behavior encourages caregivers to stay in close contact.

- ***Indiscriminate Attachment***

From six weeks to seven months, babies begin to show a preference for caregivers who are primary and secondary. They begin to think that their caregivers can meet their requirements.

While they can still accept assistance from others, babies begin to recognize the difference between people they know and those they do not and are more attentive to their primary caregiver.

- ***Discriminate Attachment***

Between around seven to eleven months old, infants display an intense affection and preferentiality for one particular person. They are prone to protest when they are removed from their primary attachment figure (separation anxiety) and will begin to exhibit anxiety around people they do not know (stranger anxiety).

- ***Multiple Attachments***

At around nine months, children begin to develop solid emotional connections with caregivers beyond their primary persona. Typically, these include parents who are not their primary caregivers, older siblings, and/or grandparents.

1.4. Why Attachment Matters

We all know that attachment is an essential component of healthy development. However, we do not know precisely why attachments are crucial, or how the process of securing attachments works.

1.4.1. Secure Attachment

Attachment happens when a child is in an established, stable mutual relationship with a loved one, usually their primary caregiver. Suppose the person caring for children's wishes has a welcoming, compassionate manner that ensures the child feels secure. In that case, the child may begin to see this person as a secure foundation from which to explore – a place of safety and security. Suppose the caregiver is readily available, responsive, and helpful during the child's the first year. In that case, the child's relationship with the caregiver will likely grow to "secure," meaning the child is confident that the caregiver is willing to assist or support them. The importance of attachment is paramount, and its impact is felt throughout our lives.

1.4.2. Benefits of Secure Attachment

Secure attachment has been associated with positive outcomes for children, which include:

- Brain Development: The brain's growth rate is rapid during the first three years of our lives. Numerous events influence the way the brain develops. When the brain is stimulated positively, it creates connections that are based on those experiences. For instance, speaking or singing to children can help build neural pathways connected to language. The effects of attachment on brain development are felt in two ways. Firstly, when a child is secure and feels cared for by a caregiver, the brain will use its energy to build pathways that are essential for higher-level thinking. Secure attachment is particularly linked to the growth of the frontal cortex in the brain, which is involved in making decisions, reasoning, and judgment. Furthermore, by creating a "home base" from which children can go out into the world and feel secure as they grow, the secure attachment allows children to experience more diverse experiences and consequently build more connections in the brain.

• Social & Emotional Development: If a child has a strong connection with their primary caregiver, they learn to trust other people, to manage and display their emotions, and learn how others will respond to their conduct. Additionally, the secure bonding process can contribute to the growth of empathy. If a child views herself as valuable and worthy of love, she is capable of seeing others in the same way. The child begins by working to satisfy her main caregiver and, as time passes, extends her attention to her classmates, siblings, friends, and community members.

- Self-Regulation: If caregivers respond to their needs, children are taught to manage their moods and behavior. If children feel stressed, stress hormones are released into the brain. If caregivers react with gentle actions, they help the child to lower their levels of these stress hormones. As time goes by, the brain develops pathways to allow this calm behavior to be activated in times of stress. So the child eventually learns to calm themselves when unhappy or angry.

1.4.3. Trauma and Attachment

Trauma resulting from neglect and child abuse can result in anxiety, fears, and the feeling of being ignored by those who are supposed to comfort the child. Since these emotional traumas are directly opposed to situations that foster attachment, it is clear that children who have a history of abuse tend to have problems with attachment. Children with a history of trauma may have various problems resulting from the lack of secure attachment. These include development problems, difficulty controlling emotions, deficient social interactions, depression, self-esteem issues, and aggressive, depressive symptoms.

1.4.4. Supporting Secure Attachment

If you are a child protection expert, you are in a unique opportunity to aid in building the bonds of trust between children and their caregivers. Here is how:

- Educate: Ensure caregivers know the meaning of secure attachment and how to create it. For example:

- Be friendly and attentive.

- Be responsive to the requirements of children.

- Children suffering from a disability need help from an adult caregiver.

- Read and respond to the signals of children.

- Enjoy time spent with dear ones (quantity is crucial).

- Participate in positive physical interaction (hugging, singing, etc.).

- Give children the opportunity to play with each other, particularly through activities that foster mutual respect.

- Provide concrete support: Stressed caregivers cannot concentrate on the needs of their children. They also are not as effective in reading or responding to signals. Giving tangible help and resources to support caregivers under stress can allow them to focus on the demands of their children. In addition, parents of younger children with little or no experience might be required to learn more about children's development and parenting. Parenting programs can assist in this area.

1.4.5. Separation and Institutionalization

Being separated from their parents and/or raised in institutions can have severe consequences for children. Bowlby pointed out that children raised in institutions are less likely to form an attachment to any adult. While the institution meets their physical needs, their emotional needs are often neglected. They are not able to bond with other infants, and then they are unable to form loving relationships as adults. Therapy interventions might be able to correct the developmental problems these children experienced. While more research is needed on this topic, it appears clear that children who bond early in life with their caregivers have a better chance of developing into well-balanced adults.

Separation from an attachment figure in childhood can lead to emotional problems. Bowlby and Robertson discovered that children who were separated from their parents while in the hospital for extended periods caused much emotional suffering. Children who were separated from their parents for too many hours lost trust in people and, like institutionalized children, were unable to build close relationships. Bowlby's efforts led to more hospitals allowing parents to remain with their children.

1.4.6. Implications for Child-Rearing

Bowlby and Ainsworth have shown that attachment is a process in which parents must do their best to determine what their children need. Parents should listen to their babies' signals and respond when they cry, laugh, or scream. Parents who respond quickly to children's signals with love and care are more likely create a secure bond with their children by the age of one. Parents should not be afraid to take the initiative and go to their children if they are not communicating. However, Bowlby stated that if parents insist on paying attention to their child, whether or not they are signaling their desire for attention, the child may become dissatisfied. Bowlby and Ainsworth believed that caretakers should be available but let the child explore their interests independently.

Chapter 2

WHY IS ATTACHMENT IMPORTANT?

2.1. The Importance of Attachment

Secure and healthy attachment is what lets your child discover the world around them and find a safe space that they can return to. Children learn to sort out their emotions and actions by looking to the person who will provide them with love and security. Attachment is crucial for long-term emotional well-being. A healthy attachment can aid your child in handling challenges as they age and may need to separate from you (such as when starting at a childcare center or school), interacting with children from other families, and developing self-control. The attachment also aids your child in developing trust with others, which is crucial to building healthy relationships later in life.

Attachment begins when the baby is born. Maternal attachment to her infant affects the baby's relationship with the mother, and the interactions between the mother and baby impact the baby's cognitive and social-emotional development. The child's attachment behavior is thought to result from emotions such as anxiety, illness, alienation or hunger, danger, and anxiety, which trigger the attachment system. These can be triggered both externally and internally. As a result of these experiences, babies develop their defenses against threats and learn physical and mental security strategies to ensure their safety and well-being.

Attachment can be described as a continuous and ongoing emotional connection most often triggered by anxiety-related tension in the relationship with the adult who takes care of the child. Kavlak (2004) states that an underlying sense of confidence results from the repeated positive bond between mother and baby. The quality of the relationship established with the attachment figure constitutes the basis for the close relations in later years.

Attachment is vital in shaping people's romantic, social and personal lives. Physical health issues (e.g., dangerous adolescent behavior) can also arise if a secure bond is not provided in infancy. The development of attachment between mother and baby begins before birth, but it is affected by a broad period that includes pregnancy, birth, and the postnatal period. Numerous conditions, including genetic ones, affect secure attachment, and healthcare professionals must be aware of these conditions in order to provide adequate support for the mother and baby.

Attachment is key in developing an emotional foundation that the child will utilize in their interactions with others throughout their life, and it can also influence how they perceive themselves. It can affect three main areas:

- The child's self-esteem

- The child's perception of other children

- A child's relationship with him or herself, as well as with other children.

Attachment can assist children in becoming more independent due to them having confidence in themselves and their caregivers. Attachment to caregivers can affect how children build bonds and interact with other children. Attachment is crucial in the development of children, and sadly, not all children have the same opportunities to develop strong attachments. Being a part of the foster system, drug abuse by caregivers, physical or mental health issues, or lack of understanding can all affect the bonds created

2.1.1. The Patterns of Attachment in Infancy and Childhood

Ainsworth studied infants' reactions to various circumstances using a technique called the Strange Situation Test. The test recorded how the infant behaved in an unfamiliar setting when they were alone, when their mother was present in the room, and when they were with a stranger. There were seven stages to the test, each which lasted for three minutes. The responses they showed when they returned to their mother were then analyzed. It was discovered that children with secure attachment showed a desire to discover and explore when they were in the room with their mothers. They also felt tension and anxiety as their mothers left, but then quickly relaxed when they saw their mothers come back into the room and were eager to share the things they found.

On the other hand, it was discovered that children with an insecure or resistant attachment pattern stopped exploring and playing once their mothers left. They were afflicted with intense tension and anxiety, and their anxiety was not reduced even when their mothers returned to the room. In addition, it was discovered that children with an insecure/resistant pattern were unable to communicate with their mother and refused to cooperate with the mother's attempts at communication after returning.

2.2. How Can You Ensure Your Baby Has a Secure Attachment?

The first signs that a strong bond is developing are among the greatest benefits parents can receive:

- At four weeks: The baby will respond to your smile,

possibly by expressing a smile or movement.

- Within three months: You will see them look at you with a smile.

- In four to six months: They will look to you and demand you address their concerns.

- In seven or eight months: They will exhibit special reactions specifically for you (they could also be angry at strangers). Your baby could also react to emotions such as sadness and anger.

If your baby is not responding to you, expressing curiosity about people, or even engaging in eye contact, you should make an appointment with your doctor.

2.2.1. Implications of Secure Attachment for Children's Development

Caregiving in the early years has a long-lasting influence on development, the capacity to learn, manage emotions, and create positive relationships (Siegel, 2012). Children who are secure with their caregivers are in a relationship based on love, stability, affection, and sensibility (Obadina, 2013). Bowlby (1974) suggested the concept of the secure base. This is the point at which children have the chance to explore, yet parents offer a safe base for them to return to in the event of becoming afraid or injured. This safe base makes the child comfortable exploring and learning.

Children with a strong bond with their caregivers are generally confident that the caregiver can provide constant reassurance and comfort them whenever they require it. They can explore the world around them as they are confident they will be able to return to their caregiver at any time and when needed (Wilkens, 2012). A caregiver's constant caring, empathy, and dedication allows the child to go through the developmental stages while developing essential self-regulation skills, comprehension, understanding, and proficiency (Kagan, 2004). Parents who are emotionally available and consistent, sensitive, and accepting enable children to build an understanding of their own psychological state, other people, and their interactions (Howe, Dooley & Hinings 2000).

Children who are able to manage their emotions perform better in school (Gottman, 1997). Secure attachments also help with mental processes that enable children to manage their emotions, lessen anxiety, be attuned to others, have a sense of self-understanding, empathy for others, and morally sound reasoning (Bath Spa University, 2014). Children with secure attachments can depend on their teachers to satisfy their requirements. In turn, they can establish strong relationships with other children, get the most out of learning possibilities, and participate in meaningful activities that require problem-solving and exploring the world. In addition, they are emotionally strong and aware of themselves. If infants develop an unbreakable bond with their parents, they are generally able to:

- Develop lasting bonds with family and friends

- Maintain emotional balance

- Feel confident in themselves

- Have fun with their friends

- Recover from disappointments and losses

- Tell others how they feel and get help when necessary.

2.2.2. Secure Attachment Bonds Are Great for Caregivers Too

Mother Nature has programmed mothers and their babies to experience the "falling in love" experience by establishing a secure bond. The joy you feel as you bond with your child will help reduce fatigue caused by a lack of sleep and the pressure of learning to take care of your child. In addition, bonding with your baby releases endorphins into your body, stimulating you, boosting your energy, and making you feel satisfied. Creating a secure bond with your baby may require work, but the benefits are enormous.

2.3. Tips for Parents to Create a Secure Attachment

It is a long-term relationship that you develop with your baby. As time passes, it becomes easier to understand the sound of the baby's cry, recognize the messages and respond to your child's needs for rest, food, love, and affection. Try to remain at peace with your child as you understand more about each other.

2.3.1. Secure Attachment Begins with Taking Good Care of Yourself

Babies communicate best when they are at peace and alert, and so are you. So however difficult it might be, looking after yourself is essential to ensure an unbreakable connection with your infant.

- Do your best to get plenty of rest: Sleep deprivation can cause you to be angry and irritable. Parents have found it beneficial to swap night duties (on two nights and away for the following two nights) or have at least one morning every week in which they can get a good night's sleep.

- Request help in the home: Especially in the infant stages, seek help wherever possible from family members, your spouse, or even your friends.

- Spend time with yourself: Caring for babies is an overwhelming task, and taking a break from the infant can help you to be a better parent. A few hours in the cafe, a stroll or yoga class, or simply doing something you want to do could give you a fresh outlook and increase your motivation.

2.3.2. Find Ways to Relax in Stressful Situations

Because babies cannot communicate verbally, they are more sensitive to the indicators of stress or anxiety. As a result, children need outside assistance to help them relax. A stressed caregiver could increase the baby's anxiety, making them more difficult to calm. If you are feeling anxious, try to find ways to relax before you engage with your child.

- Take a deep breath: Breathe deeply before putting your baby into the crib and helping them settle.

- Join forces: Do not think you must do everything by yourself. Ask for the assistance of your partner, family members, friends, or babysitters during tense moments of the day.

- Go for a walk: Fresh air and a change of scenery can help you and your child. In times of stress, try changing the environment to see if it helps you and your child relax.

Tip 1: Understand your baby's distinct signals

As many parents know, no one recipe can satisfy the demands of every baby. Each child is distinct in its particularity and preferences. The nervous system of every baby is also distinct. Some babies are soothed through sound and activity, while others prefer quiet. One of the most crucial things is to be aware of the signals your baby is sending and react accordingly. While all sounds and cries might sound similar initially, the baby may be communicating with you through sound and movement. For example, an elongated back, eyes closed tightly with fists curled, rubbing the eyes, or hyperactive or fast-paced movements all indicate specific features of your baby's emotional and physical state. Your role is to play your child's "sensory detective" and find out what they are saying to you and what you can do to respond.

- Be aware of the kinds of sounds that your baby makes and what the meaning is behind them. For instance, "I am in a frenzied state" could mean "I am hungry," whereas "I am fatigued" could be a low-pitched cry. "I am tired" may be exaggerated screaming.

- Be aware of the kind of contact your baby is most fond of and the amount of pressure they find pleasurable. Every time you touch them, your child is discovering more about the world surrounding them. Therefore, the gentler your touch, the more your child will likely find the world enticing and safe.

- Be aware of the movements, sounds, and environment your child enjoys. For example, certain babies like moving around or walking, and others react to sounds, such as gentle music, or changes in surroundings, such as when being carried outside.

- Sometimes, infants are upset regardless of external conditions, such as when they are sick, have teething issues, or are going through significant developmental changes. If this happens, continue to speak to and comfort your child. Your patience and affection will benefit them even if they are unhappy.

- Be aware of pressures from friends, loved ones, and family members. Whatever worked with one child may not be the best for your child.

Tip 2. Sleeping, eating, and the chance to create bonds of trust

Many of your baby's early indications and signs revolve around the need for rest and food. The frequency of meals or giving your baby more time to rest can hugely impact their ability to be social and engaged throughout their life. If they do not have enough sleep, babies are not capable of being at peace, and are unable to communicate with you. Babies often rest between 16 and 18 hours a day in the first few months. Exhausted infants are often extremely alert and prone to moving fast. It is possible to misinterpret this excitement as an invitation to play. However, this is your child's way of telling you that the nap time should have started. Hunger can also be the source of numerous signs your baby shows. Scheduling feeds is beneficial; however, rapid growth and developmental changes can cause your baby's needs to change over time; therefore, it is important to be attentive to the unique signals and signs.

Tip 3: Talk, play, and laugh with your baby.

Sharing your joy with your child cannot be undervalued. The joy of laughter, smiles and interaction is just as important to a child's development as sleep and food. In addition, your vocal tone and body language, as well as the way you touch your baby, are all important ways to communicate with them. If you see the signs that your child would like to play, make sure you take the time to relax and have fun exchanging smiles, fun-filled faces, and cuddles. Toys, books, and music are the perfect starting point for play. However, children with a weak nervous system may exhaust themselves quickly, so look for signs that your baby requires a break from playing as they are overwhelmed.

Tip 4: Secure attachment does not mean that parents have "perfect."

There is no need to be perfect every day to bond with your kid. Nevertheless, try your best, and do not fret if you are unsure what your child is searching for. The thing that makes a connection secure is the level and ability of your interactions with your child and your willingness to detect and fix the missed signals.

Tip 5: Do not ignore dads when it comes to secure attachment.

In families where the mother is the primary breadwinner and the father is home with the kids, the father is the baby's primary caregiver. The type of multitasking needed to look after newborns while emotionally connecting to the infant is not easy for fathers. (Information circulates more quickly through the brain's area known as the corpus callosum in women, which makes multitasking much easier). However, with effort, fathers can achieve the same outcomes.

Dads who are the primary caregivers of their child can participate in activities including:

- Feeding your baby with a bottle. As a father, you can build an emotional connection with your baby as you handle feedings and changing diapers by gazing into the baby's eyes and smiling. You can also talk to the baby while doing so.

- Reading, talking and singing with your child. Even though your baby will not know what you are saying, listening to your calm voice gives them a sense of safety.

- Playing peek-a-boo and mimicking how your baby moves.

- Impersonating the voice of your baby or making other sounds.

- Be sure to hold and touch your baby as often as possible. Keep the baby close with an infant carrier in the front, sling, or pouch during everyday activities.

- Let your baby experience various facial textures.

2.4. The Challenges of Creating a Secure Bond with Your Baby

In the ideal scenario, a secure attachment bond can be established without an issue. If, however, you or your child is suffering from a condition that hinders your ability to relax and concentrate on one another, developing a secure attachment bond could be delayed or even interrupted.

2.4.1. Babies' Challenges Can Affect the Security of Attachment

Most babies are born with the capacity to bond with their caregivers. However, there are times when babies face issues that hinder the process of developing a strong bond. For example, they can be affected by:

- Nervous system problems

- Issues during the birth

- Health issues from a young age

- Premature birth

- Being in the care of a variety of caregivers.

The earlier issues are discovered, the easier it is to fix them. If you need help, consult your pediatrician, an infant psychiatrist, or someone trained in early intervention.

Parents' own challenges can also cause problems with their children's attachment. For example, parents who did not experience a secure connection with their parents might have difficulty forming emotional connections with their infants. Other obstacles that could inhibit the bond you form with your child include:

- Anxiety, depression, or any other emotional issues

- Alcohol or drug problems

- Stress levels (from financial issues and lack of support, excessive work, etc.)

- A neglectful, abusive or chaotic childhood experience

- Living in a hazardous environment

- Negative memories of your childhood.

2.4.2. The Effects of Secure Attachment

Children with secure attachments are typically the most likely to develop strong bonds when they reach adulthood because they have already experienced the capacity to build trusting bonds, and generally feel confident that their needs are being met. A strong attachment during infancy leads to greater interaction and involvement with others, which can lead to improved communication throughout life. A secure attachment also aids children's confidence because their life experiences reinforce the belief that they are loved and cared for. This, in turn, creates a foundation that allows children to develop autonomy and explore. It can lead to confidence in school and the ability to build relationships with peers and teachers. Older kids may experience better school performance, goal-oriented behavior, and the ability to cooperate and work with their peers. A study by the *Attached Family* magazine emphasizes that a positive attachment can help avoid negative outcomes in the early years of development, including dependence, misbehavior, and over-extended demands.

2.4.3. The Effects of Insecure Attachment

Conversely, insecure attachments can affect the development of children in many ways. A Scholar Works project found that an insecure relationship can trigger many negative outcomes that manifest during childhood and frequently continue into adulthood. These include:

- Insufficient ability to socialize, problem-solve, and cope with the challenges of everyday life

- An increase in temper tantrums

- A withdrawn and emotional behavior

- Aggression.

One crucial element of children's relationships with their care-givers is how emotional connections are taught. Unfortunately, instead of showing emotions or social skills, those with weak attachments might try to attract the attention of others with their behavior or cover up their feelings completely. This type of deceit or internalization may cause anxiety, depression, and even psychopathy from a young age. In addition, it may open the way to an adolescent being afflicted by anxiety, self-esteem issues, and social rejection, creating an endless cycle.

Although it is a serious issue, insecure attachments are not unavoidable, and they do not have to alter one's life forever. Professionals in child advocacy, such as those in psychology and social work, can support interventions that can transform bad habits and collaborate with families to facilitate change by providing education to the child and the caregivers to improve their relationship over time. They can also work to bring about change at a larger level, such as developing educational programs for new parents and raising awareness about attachment's effect on childhood development.

2.5. Adults with Attachment Disorders

An attachment disorder is a disorder in the mood or behavior that hinders an individual's ability to establish and maintain relationships. The majority of these disorders develop during early childhood. They may develop in children who are unable to maintain a steady emotional connection to a parent or primary caregiver. There is no official assessment of attachment disorders for adults; however these may be due to an undiagnosed or untreated attachment disorders in the early years of childhood.

2.5.1. Different Types of Attachment Disorders

Reactive attachment disorder (RAD) typically results from maltreatment or neglect in the early years of childhood. It was observed that children suffering from RAD:

- May be unable to communicate with other people

- Show little emotion during social interactions

- Find it difficult to calm down in times of stress

- May seem unhappy, angry, or even afraid when engaging in everyday interactions with their caregivers.

If the child does not receive effective treatment, the symptoms of RAD can last until adulthood. Symptoms that could be indicative of the disorder in adults include:

- Difficulty reading emotions

- Refusal to love

- Difficulties in showing affection

- Low levels of trust

- Difficulty maintaining relationships

- Anger issues.

Disinhibited social engagement disorder (DSED) may develop as an aftermath of social neglect and a lack of a consistent connection to the primary caregiver in the initial two years of life. Children who are in care frequently exhibit signs of DSED. Symptoms include:

- Extreme social interaction

- Willingness to engage with strangers

The problem could develop or last into adulthood if a child suffering from DSED does not receive effective treatment. An adult or adolescent affected by DSED may exhibit:

- Hyperactivity

- Trust and confidence in people they do not have a good understanding of

- An inclination to ask intrusive questions to people they have only just met.

2.6. Adult Relations and Attachment Disorder

An attachment disorder that manifests during childhood can impact relationships throughout adulthood. An individual suffering from an attachment disorder might struggle with trusting others or feeling secure in the relationship. As a result, they may struggle to form and maintain romantic relationships.

2.6.1. Complications

Untreated RAD or DSED can cause the following symptoms in adulthood:

- Low self-esteem

- Emotional impairment

- Difficulties in social situations

- Substance abuse.

2.6.2. Cure

The cure for childhood attachment disorder is usually therapy. A mature adult might also consider attachment therapy or couples counseling. Attachment therapy is a method of helping people overcome negative childhood experiences of attachment. Couples therapy can assist couples in recognizing how an attachment disorder might be affecting their relationship. By gaining this information and the guidance of a therapist, couples can create strategies and tools to enhance their bond.

2.6.3. When to Visit a Doctor

Ideally, treatment should start during childhood. If a child has been the victim of any kind of neglect or abuse, they are likely to require psychotherapy, regardless of whether or not they suffer from any attachment problem. Anyone concerned that their actions or thoughts may be negatively affecting their relationships may want to talk with a doctor or a psychotherapist. Additionally, anyone who has experienced abuse could benefit from discussing the issue with a therapist. Past issues that are not resolved might be influencing present behavior and thoughts.

Conclusion

A mature adult is not likely to be diagnosed with an attachment disorder as the guidelines for clinical diagnosis only address children's issues. However, if the child with an attachment disorder fails to receive the appropriate treatment, symptoms may manifest throughout adulthood, creating difficulties in relationships and social interactions. Anyone who has been through trauma in their childhood or has been neglected ought to seek the help of a physician or psychotherapist, particularly if they feel the problem is impacting their relationships.

Chapter 3

WHAT FACTORS AFFECT ATTACHMENT?

Babies are wired to form strong emotional bonds and attachments to their caregivers. This attachment allows children to grow up trusting and confident, and capable of managing anxiety and stress. This chapter examines the definition of secure attachment and the elements that affect such a connection. It also discusses the intricacies of the attachment process and how to support this vital process for children and their parents.

3.1. Factors that Affect Attachment

Certain situations can create obstacles for children and their parents in their bid to create an established secure relationship. These may include:

- Maltreatment, abuse, and trauma

- Parental mental health difficulties

- Use of drugs by parents

- The child being in multiple care homes

- Parents who are separated from their child shortly after birth, as in the case of a baby receiving care for neonatal issues

- Anxiety, such as having a low income or being a single parent

- Loss or death of another caregiver to whom a child had an emotional connection to

3.1.1. What Factors Influence Patterns of Attachment?

The debate over nature versus nurture was among the most long-running and controversial issues of the 20th century. Are the primary traits of a person's behaviors acquired, or are they born with them? Genes define the capability to act in a particular manner; however, experiences determine how and when these capabilities are utilized. This is also the case with attachment theory. The central tenet of attachment theories is the way infants deal with stress. The frequency at which infants are affected by distress and how it manifests is determined by genetic influences; however, this behavior can be modified through education and experience. While infant characteristics influence the relationship between the caregiver and infant, the experiences provided by caregivers are the main aspect in determining the baby's attachment behaviors.

The way that parents raise their children can have a big impact on the behavior of infants with regards to attachment. Attachment classes of caregivers of infants are often established before birth, influenced by mothers' perceptions of the approaching birth of their baby. In addition, numerous studies have shown that mothers' home behavior may also predict their attachment tendencies. These findings indicate a significant impact of caregivers in the development of patterns of attachment.

3.1.2. Attachment and Caregiving

- *Parenting Styles*

Different parenting styles can influence the classification of attachment a child has with their parents. Parents who are available and sensitive to their child's signals and sensitive to their needs generally have children who feel safe around them. Contrast this with caregivers of infants who are not secure in their own attachment and tend not to be as sensitive to signals of distress and the need for protection and comfort. They are not there physically, mentally, or emotionally and can be unresponsive or unpredictable in their parenting style.

- *Sensitivity of Caregivers and Attachment Styles*

In 1972, Sylvia Bell and Mary Ainsworth investigated mothers' responsiveness to infant cries. Mothers who responded more to their infants' cries had babies that cried less and displayed more diverse vocal expressions and gestures. Researchers have attempted to reproduce these observations with mixed outcomes. Most studies provide some measurement of caregiver sensitiveness or the ability to respond to the infant's distress signals. In many instances, the definition of attachment has expanded and encompasses many elements of the bond between the infant and caregiver, as opposed to the idea that attachment is purely a security mechanism, which was the basis of the study in 1972.

A handful of studies have examined the sensitivity of mothers in specific situations. For example, one study showed that maternal sensitivity was not as high in mothers who did not have social support. Another study found that distress management by caregivers was a predictor of the security of attachment.

Most encouragement for caregiver behavior or attachment link is derived from research on infants who have a disorganized attachment to their caregivers. Caregivers who encourage disorganized attachment among their children may be unable to relieve the baby's distress as they can be an irritant to the infant. Fearful, scared, or insensitive caregiver behavior can all lead to disorganized attachment.

- *Attachment to the Caregiver*

The parental style is often a predictor of the caregiver's attachment. A review of nine studies revealed that 77% of those categorized as autonomous also had infants classified as secure. Conversely, 57% of adults who were dismissive had avoidant infants, 21% of preoccupied adults had resistant infants, and 52% of unresolved adults had disorganized infants. This suggests that parenting methods and caregivers' own experiences of attachment have a significant impact on their children's attachment.

3.2 Infant Factors

Caregivers play a crucial role in shaping patterns of attachment and behavior. However, is it the same for infants? Do the characteristics of infants influence their attachment? Some infant traits have been studied by researchers, along with the presence of medical conditions.

Infant Temperament

Temperament is a term used to describe the aspects of an infant's behavior and emotional responsiveness that are influenced by genetics. It is impossible to establish an exact gauge of temperament as the environment always influences behavior. In general, babies are more likely to show evident behavioral differences immediately following birth, which could be due to significant genetic influences. A child's threshold to express distress is a factor that affects temperament. It is a key element in attachment theories. This implies that the temperament of infants plays a part in the formation of attachment behaviors.

Theorists of temperament and attachment acknowledge that the impact of attachment is influenced by both infant and care-giver aspects. However, they differ in their importance to each of these variables. For example, they do not agree on the impor-tance of infant behavior in the Strange Situation concept. According to theorists of attachment, infant behavior can reflect a child's perception of their responsibility as a protector from prior experiences with stress.

According to theories, there are fundamental variations in infants' levels of intensity and the way they express their feelings. This is the reason for the variety of behavior observed during the Strange Situation test. When we consider the situation of infants who have a difficult time interacting with their parents, theories studying infants' temperament suggest that children in such situations have been conditioned biologically to feel relatively little emotional stress. Therefore, as per the Strange Situation test, the infants experience less stress and do not need to search for contact with caregivers.

However, there is compelling evidence to refute this idea. Research that focuses on physical and not emotional reactions to stress has found that children who experience stress exhibit the same or even as much physical stimulation as children who do not. The behaviors evident in the Strange Situation test may reveal a child's methods of managing stress, not necessarily the degree of arousal or anxiety.

- *Medical Conditions in Infants*

Children with medical conditions are typically different from healthy infants. Understanding how these conditions affect attachment can help researchers better determine how various factors affect the formation of attachment habits. Many studies have investigated the effect of various infant medical conditions on the caregiver-child relationship. Several have demonstrated that infants suffering from medical conditions tend to be more involved in less secure relationships than other children. However, another study revealed that infants' medical conditions did not affect how they bond.

3.3. Factors that Lead to a Secure Connection

The factors contributing to secure bonding between the mother and the child during the infant's two years are listed below.

- ***Spending Time Together in a Meaningful Way***

Most working mothers (89%) acknowledged that time spent with their children increases the bond between mother and child. A working mom should make an effort to spend time with their family. Sometimes, this may require sacrificing hobbies or delaying other obligations, but enhancing the time you spend with your child is the best way to create an even stronger relationship. Mothers stressed that the enjoyment of the child's involvement in activities that are important to him should be the primary factor in quality time.

In addition, children up to two years old require physical contact with their mother. Spending this time with them in a positive way creates the bond stronger. It may be difficult, but establishing an attachment bond is essential.

• *Mothers Who Solve Problems*

Working mothers said that taking on the role of problem solver was a way to establish an intense bond with their child. They believed that this role was instinctively integrated into the job of motherhood. Addressing fundamental physical needs like feeding, changing diapers, and bathing can help the attachment relationship. Infants and babies feel uncomfortable when they experience the desire to satisfy their physical needs. Most participants reported that recognizing the discomfort and reacting immediately to it results in satisfaction for the child and allows him to trust their mother to solve these concerns.

• *Breastfeeding*

Over half of mothers surveyed believed that breastfeeding was the best way to establish a bond with the baby from birth. Based on participants' opinions, breastfeeding as an emotional source is an inherent right of the child that should be protected. It provides comfort to the child and a place where he can feel at ease as he is held and fed by his mother. However, 23% of mothers in the study believed that breastfeeding alone is insufficient to create the necessary bond. The mother should take good care of herself to give her child a nutritious diet. To build a close relationship with her child, she must eat well, exercise regularly, and maintain her thoughts and personality. These traits are passed to the child through the milk of the breast. If breastfeeding is done properly, there will be no disruption to the transference process.

- ***Creating a Routine***

It is believed that keeping children on a routine improves attachment security. A routine helps the child develop the habit of organizing his daily activities. This ensures he accepts challenges easily and with a sense of understanding. It also helps the mother assign time slots to meet basic needs like sleeping, bathing, eating, etc., and playtime/social interactions with children. A routine can help arrange and manage one's time to ensure that the mother who works can meet her responsibilities while caring for the child. The mother must make time for herself outside of work. This time for herself is a source of energy, a refuel that helps her relax to take on the role of a busy mother.

- ***Mother's Protection from Emotional and Physical Abuse***

According to some, the mother figure is the strongest protector from the child's point of view; a shield against all physical and emotional harm. An attack on a child can take many forms, including being scolded or hit by family members and non-maternal caregivers.

• *Informing the Child About the Routine*

It is essential to inform the child when the mother is at work, so they are not in the dark regarding the mother's location. Making sure that the child is informed and understands the situation is a way to satisfy his curiosity and help him accept the routine. This leads to an enduring bond between the parent and the child. The participants also believed that providing the child with an understanding of morals, values, and ethics creates an effective bond. In this way, the mother's role is to share her concept of ethics and humanity. This can be taught by example or verbal coaching, as well as through storytelling. Participants felt it was essential to have the mother share these concepts since there is an emotional connection to the process.

• *Non-Maternal Caretaker Stability*

A few mothers stressed the importance of a non-maternal caregiver's stability, particularly in the case of the caregiver in charge of the baby's care when the mother is at work. Children are very vulnerable and require time to establish a connection with their caregivers. It is more calming for the child and the mother if the caretaker remains the same. Unhappy children may be reluctant to remain with the constantly changing caretakers and may become agitated. This can even affect the trust relationship that the child shares with his mother, which could disrupt their attachment.

• *Bringing Together Secure Attachment*

The primary factor in improving the relationship between the parent and child is to be responsive and sensitive in parenting. Sensitivity refers to the mother's ability to comprehend the infant's acts and vocalizations as communicative signals to indicate needs and wants, and responsiveness refers to the appropriateness of the mother's response. If, for instance, the child is sick or has a fever, a caring mother will be able to discern by his facial expressions or body temperature change and respond quickly by going to the doctor or providing over-the-counter medications. Being responsive and sensitive in parenting builds trust between the child and the mother. The child can easily turn to her for assistance and expect an appropriate response.

3.4 Genetic and Environmental Influences on Attachment at an Early Age

3.4.1. Environmental Factors

Bowlby's attachment theory is a true environmental theory since it has been able to explain different attachment patterns through individual differences in caregivers' behavior. In their groundbreaking study, Ainsworth and her colleagues discovered connections between caregiver behavior at home and the usual behavior patterns observed in the laboratory-based Strange Situation test. The researchers concluded that the most effective secure behavior pattern is associated with sensitive responses at home. Sensitivity was conceptually distinguished from responsiveness because sensitized responses can be defined by a thorough understanding of infants' communication and changing demands. The avoidant pattern may be attributed to ignoring infants' messages, particularly for signals that express negative emotions. In the context of the pattern, inconsistent, unreliable care was identified.

In the effects of non-maternal child care, researchers found higher rates of anxiety when a lower quality of maternal sensitivity was present. This study concludes that in certain situations, the non-maternal care of infants can impact security in attachment and influence the development of children.

3.4.2. Genetic Contribution to Individual Variation in Attachment of Infants

Newborns' natural arousal and distress states directly affect parents. However, theorists of attachment have suggested that temperament does not directly affect the degree of attachment since infant characteristics like temperamental issues can be accommodated by compassionate caregivers who can build secure bonds with their children. Meanwhile, temperament researchers insist that interactions between caregivers and children in the Strange Situation test reflect the infant's temperament, not the way relationships are created. In their comprehensive research, Vaughn and Bost argue that temperament and attachment are distinct concepts. Studies that prove the interrelationships between them on the one hand and separation on the other are based on different understandings and assessments of both. Nevertheless, many empirical studies have proven the connection between attachment and infant susceptibility to distress or stress regulation.

3.4.3. The Effects of Interactions Between Genes and Environment

Certain genetic influences on phenotypes can depend on particular environments and therefore may not be detected in other situations. In the same way, reaction to certain environments frequently depends on the person's genetic makeup. This interaction between environment and genes could influence individual development at the beginning of life and the development of mental health disorders. A shift from association studies focused on the main effects of genetics to studying the interplay between environmental and genetic influences can be seen in the increasing evidence of such mechanisms being reported in recent studies. New studies are being published that describe the modulation of behavioral responses to conditions for early rearing that are influenced by particular genotypes.

Genetics may also impact the relationship between childhood abuse and subsequent psychological maladaptation, particularly in the case of early maltreatment and later antisocial behavior among males. One study found that the 5-HTTLPR gene's serotonin regulatory polymorphism in the transporter gene decreased the effect of childhood trauma on depression, both in males and females. In this research, it is important to remember that the genetic factors did not significantly influence the outcome as these genetic influences were only discovered when the environmental impact of maltreatment was considered in the study.

These effects from the interaction between genes and environment on attachment coincide with Belsky's notion of the susceptibility differential, i.e., the susceptibility of children to the experience of being loved appears to depend on genetic factors. However, this research, like the majority of studies, was carried out with smaller sample sizes. These initial research studies regarding the interactions between genes and environments on attachment need to be confirmed through more comprehensive research, which could include several polymorphisms found in different candidate genes.

3.4.4. Cultural Factors

Different cultures assign different roles to the father. For example, men were traditionally expected to be the breadwinner for their families and not be involved in the care of their children. However, this stereotypical view might not be true. Although fathers were historically not involved in the day-to-day care of their children, they were involved in factors like play, instruction, and guidance. Modern Indian families are more likely than middle-class Indian families to engage in physical play with their fathers.

3.4.5. Social Policy

Until 2003, UK fathers were not allowed to take paternity leave. This meant that the mother had implicitly taken over responsibility for child care. This could affect the relationship between children and their fathers. However, this is not the case in all countries, so the attachment pattern between fathers and children may differ.

3.4.6. Biological Elements

Heerman et al. (1994) found that men seem less sensitive to infant cues than women. This was believed to be the result of certain hormones. However, Frodi et al. (1978) discovered that the physiological response of men to this phenomenon was identical to that of women.

3.5. The Interaction Between the Infant and Caregiver

Researchers studying attachment Alan Sroufe illustrated how innate characteristics of the infant, as well as caregivers of the parents, may interact to affect the way that attachment behavior is formed. While parenting style is the most important element in determining the type of attachment, infant temperament and parenting style can help determine the infant's subgroup in the main attachment group. This will be explained in greater detail in the following sections. The care provided by caregivers affects the child's degree of security, and the child's temperament determines the type of behavior that demonstrates insecurity displayed. When a child's temperament dictates the behaviors and elicits the caregiver's reaction, these actions determine how the child's natural habits develop to create a certain kind of attachment.

3.5.1. Regulation of Emotions

Regulating emotional states is the act of altering emotions to meet the requirements and needs of day-to-day life. It is through control of their emotions that babies, as well as caregivers, influence the relationship between them. In the beginning, the child's character defines the severity of their reaction to stress. Then, the caregiver's reaction to this reaction determines how the child is taught to deal with the situation. There is evidence that caregivers from three distinct categories perceive emotions differently. For instance, caregivers of infants with parents who are avoidant perceive emotional images using more eloquent descriptions different from other caregivers. This may influence the formation of attachment patterns.

The ability of caregivers to think and comprehend naturally far exceeds infants' ability. Because infants depend on their caregivers and their capacity to think, caregivers are in a place of accountability and are in charge of developing infant attachment behavior.

3.5.2. Attachment and Emotions

Babies have difficulty controlling their emotions and can easily become overwhelmed by them. They rely on their primary caregivers for guidance. Through them, the infant learns the skills necessary to be self-protected and intimate. The following are some other important functions of a secure attachment between an infant's caregiver and the child:

Learning basic trust as a foundation for all future relationships

- Developing the ability to control behavior

- Establishing a foundation for identity development, which includes self-worth and a sense of capability

- Establishing a moral framework that fosters empathy, compassion, conscience

- Creating a core set of beliefs

- Assisting with stress and trauma prevention.

3.5.3. Bidirectional Bonding and Trust

Not only do children need their family for safety and nutrition, but they also require psychosocial support, socialization, and a sense of belonging. Humans are far more concerned with their offspring than Earth's inhabitants, who tend to have webbed toes and feathered wings. We do not force fledglings to leave the nest after 21 days or before fertilized eggs turn into tadpoles. According to evolution, humans generally have babies when it is safest to do so. Although a baby's brain still needs years to develop, it is typically born when it is safe. The baby relies on its parents or guardians for protection, food, and care until the brain matures sufficiently.

Skin-to-skin bonding can help babies regulate their temperature, heart rate, and stress hormone levels, and improve immunity. Babies in orphanages, which are biologically cared for – fed and cleaned – can die from lack of human touch. All children need to feel loved and connected to their caregivers. Although "bonding" can be unidirectional (e.g., parents showing affection to an unborn child), "attachment" is bidirectional. It is formed through interactions between children and caregivers and builds trust. Children and babies learn to trust adults by having their needs met. Adults should be trustworthy. Hormonal and psychological connections in young brains can be broken if something bad happens. It can take years to repair the damaged psyche if the foundation of trust and security is broken.

PART 2 – WHAT IS MY ATTACHMENT STYLE?

Chapter 4

SECURE ATTACHMENT

4.1. What is Secure Attachment?

Secure attachment is the most prevalent kind of attachment in Western society. According to research, 66% of all US people are securely attracted. People who develop this kind of attachment are happy, warm, social, and easy to get to know. They can express their emotions. They also tend to form profound, meaningful, and lasting relationships. Adults who have secure attachments are also generally well-liked in the workplace. Parents who wish to ensure that their children are secure could benefit from studying the subject and working out any issues they face with their own attachments.

4.1.1. How Do We Define Attachment Theory?

Many people joke that if they go to a therapist, they will be asked questions regarding their past. Although it is not always the case, this is the case in the case of a therapist to address issues with your relationship. According to psychoanalyst and psychiatrist John Bowlby, our first relationships with our families (or caregivers) determine how we think and behave in all relationships we have throughout our lives. Why is this so? We depend on our parents or primary caregivers as children and infants. We rely on them for survival and are forced to be attached to them and trust them to take good care of us.

Most parents will try their best to meet their children's requirements and give them the warmest and most loving environment possible. Suppose they are attuned and attentive to our needs. In that case, we can establish an unshakeable and steady connection with them, which creates the ability to develop a secure attachment to life. However, if our needs are not being met, or if we feel that our needs are not satisfied, we are likely to create one of the three attachment types classified as insecure. Although it is easier to establish an enduring attachment bond with a newborn, it is possible to build a relationship at any age. This will ensure that your child has the best start in life.

4.1.2. What Is the Attachment Bond, and Why Is It Crucial?

An attachment bond is an emotional connection resulting from the lack of communication between a baby and their primary caregiver or parent. The attachment bond is not dependent on the level of affection you have for your child but rather on the emotional connection you establish in your relationship with your baby. Attachment happens naturally when you, as the caretaker or parent, take care of your child's requirements; however, the quality of the bond between you and your child varies.

- Secure attachment bonds will ensure your child feels safe, secure, and understood. Secure bonds will allow him or her to develop his nervous system effectively. As a result, your child's brain develops and can organize itself, leading to self-awareness, compassion, trust, and learning.

- Insecure attachment bonds are formed when you do not meet your child's basic needs for safety, understanding, and peace. This can hinder the development of your child's brain, leading to problems later in life with learning and relationships, as well as mental and emotional development.

4.2. How Are Secure Attachments Formed?

When a baby arrives, they naturally anticipate that their caregivers can meet their needs. The baby utilizes physical signals (such as crying) to inform caregivers of a problem and hopes they will deal with it. Parents who raise their children in a secure attachment do not break their trust. Nevertheless, it is not necessarily as simple as it appears. Making sure you have an enduring attachment bond with your child and giving them the most positive possible start in life does not require you to be a perfect parent. The 2000 study revealed that the most important aspect of the child-primary caregiver relationship was not the quality of care, education, or bond between parents and infants. Instead, it depends upon the quality of non-verbal communication between you and your baby.

As your child grows up, it is easy to build trust. Children's brains continue to grow well into adulthood, even into their 20s. It is never too late to develop an emotional non-verbal relationship with your child, as the brain's structure is constantly changing. You can improve your non-verbal communication skills to help people connect with you regardless of age.

4.2.1. The Bond of Attachment Is Different from the Love Bond

As a parent or primary caregiver, you can follow the guidelines for parenting and provide loving, 24/7 support for your child, but you will not necessarily be able to establish an enduring bond with your child. You can attend to your child's physical needs and ensure the coziest home with the finest quality of food, the most enlightened education, and every other material thing children could ever want. You can cuddle, hug and love your child, but not create an environment that encourages optimal growth for your child. What is the way to do this? Most importantly, making a secure attachment differs from creating a love bond.

Children need more than love and care to allow their brains and nervous systems to function at their best. Children should be able to communicate their emotions in a non-verbal way with their primary caregiver. This will help them feel loved, secure, and at peace. Children who feel emotionally distant from their primary caregivers are likely to feel anxious, confused, and insecure, no matter how much they love them.

Bonding: Secure Attachment Bond

- Bonding with your child starts before birth and generally develops quickly during the first few weeks after the baby's birth.

- The emotional bond with you keeps growing throughout his or her life.

- You must be attentive to your child's needs, whether that is changing their diapers, feeding them, or going to soccer practice or to watch a film.

- Pay attention to what is happening at this moment in the relationship between your child and yourself. For instance, do your child's nonverbal signals indicate that they are discontented? Do you acknowledge this?

- Follow your child's slower speed and react to non-verbal signals, such as, "I am in no hurry; I am having fun just hanging out with you."

- Engage your child in conversation whenever possible. Ask them about their favorite meals or what is going on at school.

- Remain "in the moment." Talk, listen, play and give the child your complete attention, with no distractions.

Attachment and Love in Adulthood

For several years, researchers have investigated the cognitive, affective, and behavioral responses of persons with various adult romantic attachment orientations to various stressful settings. As mentioned earlier, Bowlby said that attachment motivations impact how individuals think, feel, and act in intimate relationships "from the cradle to the grave," even though the attachment system is most evident in young children. He argued that this was since attachment motivations influence how individuals learn to manage their emotions and conduct in intimate relationships. Despite this, the attachment system is more evident in the conduct of infants and young children. Following in their footsteps, attachment insecurity may be seen as a disease that can lead to the development of maladaptive interpersonal behaviors when certain stressful or harmful situations occur. This is consistent with the initial conception of the disorder.

The major objective of the behavioral attachment system is to increase the likelihood that susceptible people will survive the inherent dangers of the baby's development period. As a direct result of natural selection, the attachment system is designed to become active (activated) anytime a person feels fear, anxiety, or any other discomfort. From an evolutionary standpoint, the system's purpose is to increase the likelihood of survival by keeping fragile infants, children, and adults in continual contact with their parents (or other caring figures). Since intimacy lessens feelings of dread, fear, and other associated pain, people can concentrate on other aspects of their lives. When people feel a significant drop in their levels of fear, concern, or discomfort, the disintegration of the attachment system happens (ie., it shuts off).

Throughout their development, individuals maintain a mental record of the extent to which they can get enough closeness and comfort from the attachment figures in their life. Their parents are listed first, followed by their close friends and romantic relationships. This data is used to establish if a person is emotionally secure. These mental representations, also known as working models, consist of two parts: (1) a model of significant others (such as parents, close friends, or romantic partners), which includes information about their responsiveness to one's bids for proximity or comfort in previous interactions; and (2) a model of the self, which includes information about one's ability to achieve sufficient proximity or comfort and one's value as a relationship partner. Using operational models, individuals are assisted in deciding how they want to act in any given situation.

Bowlby believed that the way a person is treated by significant people throughout their lives, especially in times of difficulty, is the most influential element in defining their expectations, attitudes, and beliefs towards future partners and relationships. Individuals' expectations, attitudes, and beliefs function as "if-then" statements that govern their thoughts, emotions, and actions, especially when disrupted. This is particularly true when expectations are not realized (for example, "If I am upset, then I can count on my partner to support me."). These statements affect the ideas, emotions, and behaviors of individuals. After they have been formed, functional models regulate how people interact with their interpersonal environment, including their intimate relationships, particularly in stressful or potentially dangerous circumstances. Nevertheless, models that are now in use may change over time in response to new experiences or events that sharply contradict their assumptions. This may occur as a result of the passage of time.

Attachment patterns in adult romantic relationships may be split into two main categories: adult-child and adult-adult. The degree to which people feel at peace with the amount of physical closeness and emotional intimacy in their romantic relationships is reflected by the first factor, avoidance. Extremely avoidant individuals have unfavorable perceptions of potential romantic partners and generally have good views of themselves, even though these views may sometimes be fragile. Avoidant people mistakenly believe that attempting to establish a psychological and emotional connection with their love partners is either impossible or undesirable. As a direct result, they place a premium on establishing and maintaining their independence, control, and autonomy within the framework of their romantic relationships. People who engage in avoidant behavior are motivated by these ideals to utilize distancing and deactivating coping strategies, which require them to intentionally suppress negative thoughts and emotions to promote autonomy and independence. These individuals also engage in avoidant conduct because they feel this will allow them to manage their lives. People with a low avoidance score are firmly attached because they are comfortable with intimacy and are willing to depend on others and be depended on by others. They have a low avoidance score because they are comfortable with closeness and are willing to rely on others.

The second factor, known as worry, measures the extent to which people are concerned that their love partners will not value them enough or will leave them. High-anxiety individuals have a strong need for a deeper emotional connection with their partners, and as a consequence, they devote a considerable deal of time and effort to nurturing their romantic relationships. People battling anxiety are more likely to have unfavorable perceptions of themselves and cautiously optimistic views of their love relationships. Anxious individuals have a propensity to question their worth, fear losing their relationships, and stay hypervigilant for any signs that their partners may be moving away. Due to these inconsistent sensations, anxious individuals tend to question their validity. As a result, they are motivated by the urge to enhance their insufficient sense of imagined security, causing them to act in ways that might sometimes suffocate or drive away their relationships.

As a result, people are compelled to enhance their insufficient sense of imagined security. Anxiety sufferers tend to develop mental models that compound their suffering, causing them to feel even more insecure. This is because anxious persons are uncertain as to whether or not they can rely on the relationships they have. Anxiety-afflicted individuals tend to rely on emotionally focused and hyperactive coping strategies when in discomfort. These strategies either maintain or increase the anxious individual's concerns and anxieties and often keep the anxious individual's attachment systems engaged continuously. This partially explains why nervous persons often have relationships that are both less fun and more suited to their needs. People with a low anxiety level (those who are more securely bonded to others) lack these persistent anxieties and concerns. These individuals have a low level of anxiousness. Gender seldom interacts with attachment anxiety or avoidance to predict the outcomes of partnerships. Although some surveys indicate that women have somewhat higher anxiety scores and males have slightly higher avoidance scores, these gender differences are essentially insignificant.

4.2.2. The Confusion Surrounding Bonding and the Secure Attachment Bond

The term "bond" is often used to refer to both the caretaking process and the relationship that is part of the attachment process, although they are very different methods of connecting with your child. One relies on the amount of care parents provide to their infant child, and the other is based on the nature of non-verbal emotional communication between the parent and the child.

The two types of interaction between parents and children can occur in tandem. For example, when bathing, feeding, or otherwise taking care of the child in your care, you may also develop a bond by being aware of and reacting to your child's nonverbal signals.

Before scientists understood the profound changes happening in the infant's brain in the first few months, the years following the caretaking and attachment processes were considered the same. Today, however, they can observe and meticulously document the infant's nonverbal behaviors to reveal infant attachment processes.

4.2.3. Milestones That Relate to Secure Attachment

When you understand the milestones in development that are related to secure attachment, you can identify signs of a weak attachment and then take the necessary measures to correct them immediately. If your child is missing frequent milestones, it is crucial to speak with an experienced pediatric doctor or a child developmental specialist.

Between birth and 3 months, your baby is expected to...

- React and follow vibrant colors, movements, and even objects

- Turn towards a sound

- Pay attention to the faces of others

- Smile at you when you smile.

Between three and six months, your baby is expected to...

- Be joyful when you interact with them

- Make sounds like crying or babbling to let people know they're happy or sad

- Have fun and smile often during playtime.

Between four and ten months, your baby will...

- Make use of facial expressions and sounds when you interact, such as smiling, laughing, or babbling

- Enjoy a fun exchange with you

- Alternate back and forth between motions (giving and taking), sounds, and smiles.

Between 10-18 months, your child...

- Will play games with you, such as peek-a-boo or Pattycake

- Use various gestures (sometimes in succession) to communicate needs, such as gestures of giving, pointing, or waving

- Recognize their name when you call.

Between 18 and 20 months, your baby will...

- Learn and comprehend at least 10 words

- Utilize a minimum of four consonants when babbling, for example, B D M, N, P, and T

- Make use of gestures and words to convey their requirements, such as pointing at something

- Show familiarity with individuals and body parts by gestures or looking at them when they are mentioned.

At 24 months, your baby will...

- Know and comprehend at least 50 words

- Make use of two words to express something, such as "want milk" or "more crackers."

- Play more elaborate pretend games

- Play with other children and share toys and objects

- Ask questions about familiar objects and people.

At 36 months, the baby will...

- Combine actions and thoughts, such as "sleepy, want a blanket," or "hungry for yogurt" and going to the fridge

- Play and have conversations with other children

- Discuss emotions, feelings, and interests, and demonstrate the knowledge of the time (past and future)

- Respond to "who," "what," "when," and "where" questions without too much difficulty.

4.2.4. The Obstacles to Establishing a Secure Attachment Bond

When your baby is an infant, you may notice the obstacles preventing you from forming an unbreakable relationship. While you may love your child deeply, it can be challenging to meet the needs of their developing nervous system. Infants cannot calm down and stay calm on their own, so they depend on you. It will be difficult for you to calm and soothe your infant if you cannot control your stress levels amid all the pressures and stress of everyday life. Even older children will view you as a source of security, connection, and eventually secure attachment. As a result, you may often find yourself stressed, depressed or angry, or unable to be calm or attentive to your child's emotional, physical, or cognitive development. Non-verbal communication between the child and the primary caregiver can also be impaired if either party has medical problems. This could impact the secure attachment bond.

4.5. How a Child's Health Affects the Attachment Bond

The brain is formed by experience, particularly in infants whose brains are mostly undeveloped.

- If a child experiences difficulties during pregnancy or birth, their nervous system might be affected.

- Adopted children or those who are in neonatal units

of hospitals away from their parents may be left feeling anxious or confused. They may also feel unsafe and uneasy.

- Infants who cannot cease crying, whose eyes are closed at all times with fists locked and bodies stiff, may have trouble hearing the soothing signals of a highly attuned caregiver.

As an infant's brain is influenced by experiences, the child can overcome any issues from birth. It could take several months. However, when the primary caregiver remains composed, calm, observant, persevering, and patient, the child can eventually become calm enough to allow trust to develop.

4.5.1. How a Child's Health Can Impact Attachment

The environment and experiences of a child influences their ability to develop an attachment bond. Sometimes, the conditions that impact the bond of secure attachment cannot be avoided however the child is still too young to comprehend what occurred and why. As a result, a child begins to lose trust in their surroundings, and the world turns into an unsafe place. This can happen when:

- Sometimes, the child's requirements are fulfilled, but sometimes they are not. The child is not sure what to expect

- The child is in a hospital or removed from their parents

- A child is moved from one caretaker to another (which can result from foster care, adoption, or the parent's death).

- A child is maltreated or even abused.

4.5.2. The Health of the Caretaker's Will Affect the Strength of the Bond

Your child's brain development can be affected by the emotions you experience as the primary caregiver. You might not be able to provide positive emotional mirroring to your child if you are anxious, depressed, or traumatized. Sometimes, even the most caring, healthy, and responsible caregiver might struggle to establish a secure attachment bond with their children. As a young child, you may not have had an enduring attachment bond with your principal caregiver, so you might not know what a secure bond looks like. However, adults can improve their lives too. As you strengthen your self-esteem, you can manage anxiety and emotions that could hinder your ability to form an enduring bond with your child.

4.5.3. Distractions

Mobile phones, computers, television, and other devices that are part of everyday life can keep you from focusing on your children. Answering an urgent email at lunch, texting with an acquaintance during playtime, or zoning out watching TV while your children play are just a few ways parents lose chances to engage in eye contact with their children and to engage in the secure bonding process. If you do not pay attention to your child, you will miss their non-verbal signals.

4.5.4. Secure Attachment Is Always Possible

It is always possible to strengthen and repair secure attachments, as the brain is constantly changing. If you sense a problem exists, you can correct the situation by trying to understand what your child needs for a secure attachment. This can strengthen your relationship, increase trust and resilience, and strengthen your bond.

4.6. Non-verbal Communication Techniques for Secure Attachment

Non-verbal cues are sensory signals communicated through a specific speech sound, object, or facial expression. The primary caregiver for a child integrates all these characteristics to provide a feeling of security, recognition, and security for children. Even once a child is old enough to speak, non-verbal communication is essential to establishing and maintaining a strong bond.

- Look into the eyes with affection: When you show your child love and affection, they feel a positive vibe and can feel secure, happy, and relaxed. On the other hand, you might feel sad, depressed, stressed, or distracted and unable to look into your child's eyes. Eye contact is crucial for maintaining a connection with your child.

- Facial expression: Your child's face can convey various emotions without saying one word. Therefore, they will feel safe if you are calm and focused when communicating with your children. However, if you look anxious, angry, scared or sad, scared, or distracted, your child will be able to sense these negative feelings and become anxious, insecure, and uneasy.

- Tone: Even if your child is not old enough to comprehend the language you are using, they will recognize the difference between a tone that is unfriendly, harsh, or distracted or a tone that conveys warmth, enthusiasm, concern, and understanding. When speaking to older children, ensure that your tone is compatible with the words you are using.

- Touch: Touch can reveal your state of mind, such as whether you are at peace, calm and gentle, angry, discontented, or unavailable. Your emotional state can be communicated through how you carry, wash or lift your child, and how you them with a warm hug, gentle stroke, or pat on the head.

- Body language: This is another way to communicate information to your children. If you engage your children with your hands crossed and your head tilted back, they will perceive your posture as defensive and uninterested. If you sit with your back straight, keep your eyes open and your head pointing toward your child, they will sense that their words are important to you.

- Timing, pace, and intensity: The pacing, timing, and intensity of your words and facial expressions can reveal your mental state. If you are moving at a high pace or are feeling unfocused or stressed, your non-verbal behavior will not likely help ease or calm your child. It is important to keep an eye on your child's preference for pace and intensity. These tend to be less sluggish and less intense than your personal preferences.

4.7. The Five Conditions that are Essential to Raising a Child with a Secure Attachment

There are five essential conditions you should consider if you want to raise children in a safe attachment manner.

The child feels secure.

The child should always feel safe and secure. Security means being close to their mother since she provides warmth, food, and protection for toddlers and infants. The word "danger" means being separated from her. The attuned mother is fiercely protective yet not overwhelming, disruptive, or indifferent. She allows her child to have the space and freedom to explore the universe; however, she is close enough to ensure that the child feels secure. If the baby wanders from the path and is scared, they know they can run towards her and be wrapped in a warm hug and secure against the world. This sends a signal: "You are safe. You are valued. You are loved."

The child feels loved.

Attuned parents can precisely recognize their child's signals and respond to the baby's needs. When children declare a need, they can anticipate a quick, reliable, and exact response. The result for the baby is a sense that they have control of their life from the beginning:

- If I let my family know that I am hungry, I am fed.

- If I tell my family that I am tired, my caregiver puts me down to sleep, and I will be able to rest.

- If I let my caregiver know my distress, my caregiver calms me down.

The child is comforted and reassured.

The arms of the attuned parent are wide and welcoming. Suppose the child is upset; the caregiver comforts and helps the child return to a calm and peaceful state. As time passes, the child will gain the capacity to handle the stress independently and self-soothe.

The child feels appreciated.

Being valued is a natural part of childhood and is the basis of positive self-esteem. Parents who raise their children with healthy self-esteem regularly declare their happiness about their child's identity rather than what they do. They place more emphasis on being than doing. Parents who show "expressed delight" to the child are enthralled by everything their child does. They do not focus on their chores but on the joy of being parents.

The child is supported and encouraged to explore.

Finally, children must be able to feel safe and supported in exploring their world safely and joyfully. Parents who advocate for this believe deeply in their children and give them an insurance policy. So involved in their child's development, parents give their children the space to grow and push them toward autonomy and independence. This feeling of security permits the child to explore, learn about the world, fail, and succeed. Through this exploration, children develop an independent, good, solid, unique identity.

As predictable as is possible for the child

Let us get back to the idea of not breaking your child's faith in the trust. The answer to this question is not in the particulars. However, it is in your overall approach to parenting. A minor mistake now and then is not likely to make your child insecurely connected to you. There are some things you may be looking to target. Lack of consistency (in parents) is among the main risk factors for developing insecure attachment styles (in youngsters). Do not change your approach frequently. Knowing what is expected gives your child a sense of peace and stability. It is not a good idea for the child to be constantly anxious.

Another major risk for developing an insecure bond with your child is not being conscious of your feelings and desires. If you are insecure about your attachment type, you will likely transmit it to the next generation. Suppose you think you may have issues with attachment. In that case, it might be a good idea to understand this with the help of a therapist, self-help guides, and online courses. Last but not least, keep your cool. There is no need to worry over every aspect of your parenting or your relationship with your child. Secure attachment is about your child's trust and confidence in you and your affection.

4.8. Ten Indicators that a Secure Bond Is Present in Relationships With Adults.

- Ability to control emotions and feelings during relationships

- Goal-oriented behavior that is strong when you are working on your own

- Being excellent at bonding, expressing openness to, and trusting others

- Being aware of what you are in your life and the purpose you would like to achieve

- Ability to communicate your needs effectively

- Feeling as if you have influenced the world

- At ease with intimacy and mutual dependence

- Ability to get emotional support from your partner and offer emotional assistance to your partner.

- It is a good feeling to be alone and take the time to explore

- The ability to reflect on the way you are being treated in the context of a relationship

4.8.1. Three Signs to Look For in Secure Adult Relationships

Adults with a strong attachment style tend to be more relaxed in social interactions, bonding, or intimate connections. They are conscious of their feelings and emotional requirements and can feel and express them. They are honest and open and do not take things to extremes.

A positive outlook on oneself

Securely connected adults have an optimistic image of themselves. They do not require reassurance to feel loved or worthy of affection. Nevertheless, that does not necessarily mean they are not interested in intimacy or emotional connection. Instead, they are as happy in their own skin as they are in relationships.

A positive attitude towards others

These people are also generally positive in their opinions of other people. They generally are affixed to their spouses and do not question the intentions of their loved ones. They can make gestures of affection without being in a state of confusion or fear. People who have a secure attachment style are usually loving, warm and affectionate. They are capable of establishing and maintaining lasting, meaningful romantic relationships. They are at ease with closeness and easily bond with others.

A positive perspective of childhood

Securely connected adults are also more likely to have a positive impression of their childhood. They can look back and gain a sense of their experiences in the past, even if their past was not perfect. They can appreciate the positive and can learn from bad experiences.

If you are in line with the abovementioned characteristics, you ought to consider taking a moment to be happy about that. If you think your style of attachment is not completely secure, you may be thinking about how you could alter it and make it secure. Thankfully, you can develop secure attachments as you mature.

4.9. Secure Attachment Characteristics

Children with a strong bond tend to become distressed when their caregivers are gone and ecstatic when they see their parents again. If they are scared, they will seek comfort from their parents or caregiver. Children who feel secure and attached to their parents are more likely to accept contact from them. They also welcome the parent's return with a positive attitude. They may accept comfort from people other than their parents, however, they prefer their parents to strangers. People with secure attachment are more likely to have fun with their children. In addition, they are more responsive to their children's needs and are generally more patient with their children than less secure parents. Studies have demonstrated that securely attached children are more empathic in later phases of their childhood. They are also less aggressive, less disruptive, and more mature than ambivalent or avoidant attachment types.

Although developing a secure connection to caregivers is normal and expected, as Hazan and Shaver have observed, it is not always the case. Researchers have discovered various aspects that affect the formation (or the absence) of secure bonds, especially the mother's ability to respond to the needs of her child during the first year of life. Mothers who are inconsistent in their responses or interfere with their child's playtime tend to create less active children who cry more often, and feel more stressed. Mothers who repeatedly refuse to listen or do not acknowledge their infant's requirements tend to create children who seek to avoid contact with their own infants later in life. Securely attached people are more likely to be build successful long-term relationships as they get older. Attached people also have high self-esteem, a desire to be close with others, seek social support, and can communicate their feelings. In a study that Hazan and Shaver conducted, 56% of respondents described themselves as secure, while 25% categorized themselves as avoidant, and 19% classified themselves identified themselves as anxious or ambivalent.

4.9.1. Early Intervention: Implications

Intervention for infant-caregiver relations in crisis is a key strategy to promote development and prevent longitudinal developmental disruption. It is becoming increasingly clear that infant-caregiver relationships are crucial in establishing vulnerability to various mental disorders. Research shows that early intervention in infant-caregiver conflicts should be effective at all levels. This includes neurobiological and psychological domains. It can also have implications for the overall outcome of resilience and stress regulation. These domains can be addressed psychologically and are called neuro-protective. Early intervention is possible if we identify and target children and infants at greatest risk based on caregiver vulnerability. Early intervention services should prioritize caregivers with a history of abuse, maltreatment, personality disorders, or other difficulties.

Swain and his colleagues examined the brain networks that support caregiving in humans and animals. They suggest that caregiving requires integration of the neural circuitry that underpins emotion and motivation and cognitive faculties such as attention and decision-making. These impairments can have a direct impact on the care of infants if caregivers have suffered early adversity. When addressing caregiver-child interactions, it is important to consider caregiver history. The focus should be on improving the caregiver's ability to empathize with the infant.

Psychodynamic methods are based on understanding the impact of the caregiver's past on their current interactions with their infant. The main clinical concern for traumatized caregivers is often how to reintegrate traumatized feelings and experiences. Attachment-related trauma suffered by caregivers may respond well to techniques that control anger and encourage more adaptive ways of managing adverse effect states. Others will require more intensive individual therapy that can be focused on resolving trauma from the past. For infant development, the reflective ability of caregivers is essential. Reflective caregivers can reflect and think about the inner world of their infants and help them develop self-regulation. Most infant-caregiver psychotherapy methods are designed to improve caregivers' reflective abilities. These methods also aim to connect traumatized caregivers, their current issues, and the children. Slade describes the main components of a reflective program for caregiving:

- Developing a reflective mindset.

- Modeling reflections - the caregiver represents the child's mental state to him/her.

- Facilitating wondering - The caregiver helps the child imagine their experience.

- Using affect to mentalize - using emotions to think

about the responses.

These processes revolve around the caregiver's support by a clinician, who accurately reflects on the caregiver's emotions, fears, and distress. This is especially important for traumatized mothers, whose childhood experiences may not have been validated and who are having difficulties with trust and attachment. In addition, reflective caregiving programs may be crucial to effecting change in high-risk relationships where behavioral/cognitive approaches are ineffective. This process is centered on supporting caregivers' ability to understand and manage their feelings and allowing them to tell their stories about their trauma.

Several clinical approaches focus on attachment and caregiving. These frameworks can help caregivers better understand the child's attachment needs. However, the extent to which caregivers and infants interact directly and how they do so can vary. The WWW approach instructs caregivers to watch their children engage in self-directed play and to only participate when the child initiates it. In order to help the caregiver develop awareness and understanding of the relational themes that emerge from the child's play, the therapist will discuss the session with them. The WWW approach is proven to help the child develop a more secure and organized attachment. It also increases caregiver competence and improves both infant and maternal mental health. Another issue to consider is whether caregiver-infant psychotherapy should precede individual psychotherapy. Caregivers who have experienced early relational trauma may have difficulty conceptualizing the self and the other person in relationships. This could make it difficult for them to think about the care of their infant without first working through their issues. More research is needed to study infants' representation by caregivers who have experienced early trauma or disturbances in early interaction.

Caregiving interventions for high-risk groups have been mostly behavioral. In some cases, psych-education has been added to help with attachment behaviors and the role that the attachment figure plays in some cases. Emerging research suggests that attachment-based approaches that focus on improving caregiver-infant relationships may be optimal for child development, neurobiological support organization, and emerging systems of interpersonal regulation and functioning. The effectiveness of caregiver-based interventions that aim to improve caregivers' ability to recognize and respond appropriately to young children's distress signals has increased HPA axis function and behavioral functioning in those who have experienced early adversity. The neuro-protective role of early emotion-focused attachment interventions in promoting resilience via the regulation of stress response systems is further highlighted by the more complex understanding of the effects of early life stress on HPA function and the risk of mental disorders.

Conclusion

The bonds between infants and their primary caregivers start through one-to-one interactions in the early years of birth. These interactions affect the brain, creating patterns that guide how children develop relationships as they grow older. The brains of infants that establish secure bonds have a stronger foundation or ability to create healthy relationships. Conversely, children with attachments that are negative or insecure may struggle to form healthy relationships. Building a secure connection with your child through non-verbal emotional cues such as soothing touches, attentive eye contact, and a warm and affectionate vocal tone is possible.

Chapter 5

INSECURE ATTACHMENT

5.1. What Is Insecure Attachment?

An insecure attachment style can be described as a method of dealing with relationships characterized by uncertainty or fear. A variety of different attachment types that can be described as insecure make it difficult for individuals to form profound emotional and intimate connections with their partner. "An individual who has an insecure attachment to another typically feels anxious about the relationship and whether or not the other person can meet their own needs or desires," says holistic psychologist Nicole Lippman-Barile Ph.D. They may expect the person to abandon or hurt them somehow. Insecure attachment is a broad term used to define all types of attachments that do not conform to a secure attachment style. The three kinds of insecure attachments are fearful, anxious, and fearful-avoidant. Youngsters are also referred to as ambivalent, avoidant, and unorganized.

5.1.1. Types of Insecure Attachments

- Anxious attachment: Also called the anxious-ambivalent attachment type, it is characterized by insecurity and anxiety regarding relationships. These people can be preoccupied with worries and are clingy and in need of validation and reassurance.

- Avoidant Attachment: Also known as the anxious-avoidant attachment style, it is defined by disapproving behavior. They avoid emotional intimacy and intimacy and are often unable to seek assistance.

- Avoidant fearful attachment: Also known as disorganized attachment style, this is characterized by volatile and unpredictable behavior. People who suffer from this disorder do not have effective coping strategies and cannot deal with issues in relationships.

- Anxious-disorganized attachment refers to inconsistency and difficulty trusting others.

5.1.2. What Is the Cause of Insecure Attachment?

The attachment styles develop throughout childhood and are shaped by the caregiver-child relationship. "It is essentially how we were emotionally cared for – or not cared for – as children growing up," Lippman-Barile describes. As a result, people with insecure attachment styles often have trouble establishing stability, reliability, security, and safety in their early childhood years. There are a variety of reasons why even a conscientious, loving parent might not successfully establish a secure relationship with a child. The reasons for your insecure attachment might be due to:

A mom who is inexperienced, young, or lacks the necessary parenting skills

The caregiver may have suffered from depression caused by loneliness, lack of support, or hormonal issues. A primary caregiver's addiction to alcohol or other drugs also reduces their ability to accurately detect and respond to physical or emotional needs.

- Traumatizing experiences include an accident or illness that disrupted the attachment process.

- Neglect of physical needs such as inadequate nutrition, exercise insufficiency, or disregard for medical problems.

- Abuse or neglect of the emotional: For instance, your caretaker did not focus on you when you were a child, made little effort to comprehend your feelings, or inflicted verbal violence.

- Sexual or physical assault

- Disconnection from the primary caretaker due to

death, illness, divorce, or adoption.

- Inconsistency in your primary caretaker: You may have had a series of nannies or staff members at daycare centers, for instance.

Multiple changes or moves. You may have experienced multiple environmental changes due to a childhood in foster homes.

Examples of insecure childhood behaviors:

- Clinginess

- Avoiding caregivers

- Crying inconsolably

- Repressing or hiding emotions

- Feeling anxious or upset when parents leave

- Appearing independent, but secretly wanting attention

- Fear of exploration, particularly in a completely new environment

- Insufficient emotional regulation

Examples of insecure adult behavior

- Low self-worth and self-esteem

- Frustrations with seeking assistance

- Refusal to let others go

- Fear of being abandoned

- Emotional dependence

- Aversion to intimacy

- Continuously looking for reassurance in relationships

- Being afraid of and irritated by the independence of a
  partner

5.2. How Does Insecure Attachment Affect Adulthood?

"Typically, these attachment styles (if unresolved) play out in adulthood," Lippman-Barile states. Being insecure as a child looks similar to being insecure as an adult in that the anxiety and fear of abandonment are still present. A child securely attached to their caregiver is more likely to be in a relationship with the person they love later. In the same way, a child who discovers that they cannot depend on their caregiver could be unable to trust a friend in the future. No matter how the relationship is conducted, someone with an insecure attachment might not be able to feel comfortable within the relationship. In addition to affecting relationships with romantic partners, an insecure attachment may also cause insufficient emotional control and depression, anxiety, and low self-worth.

5.3. How Do You Fix an Insecure Attachment?

To recover, it is important to know your attachment style. It might be beneficial to assess the type of insecure attachment style you are experiencing, whether it is fearful, avoidant, or fearful-avoidant. "Knowing why it may have developed and how is helpful so you can start to work on these feelings and behaviors in your relationship," Lippman-Barile explains. Therapy can help individuals identify the root causes, develop new coping strategies, and become more aware of their feelings, thoughts, and desires. Making sure you have healthy and supportive relationships is crucial, whether with family members, friends, mentors, or the person you are with. "Working with your partner and communicating this is helpful so that you both are mindful of these patterns and have a strategy to work on them," Lippman-Barile suggests. To build a strong relationship, she suggests that each partner must believe in each other and feel secure as an individual. Although people cannot change how they were raised, it is possible to create healthy strategies for coping in adulthood. Knowing a person's attachment patterns could represent the initial step in this process.

5.3.1. Help for Insecure Attachment

Suppose you can identify an insecure attachment style within yourself or your partner. In that case, you don't need to be content with accepting the same attitude, expectations, or behavior patterns throughout your life. Instead, you can change and build a more secure bonding style in your adult years. Therapy is beneficial, as is couples counseling. An experienced therapist familiar with attachment theory can assist you in understanding the meaning of your past and build a sense of security. If you cannot access the right therapy, however, there are many ways you can work by yourself to create a more secure attachment style. First, start by learning all you can about your insecure attachment style. The more you learn, the more you will be capable of recognizing and correcting the habits and reflexive behaviors of an insecure attachment style that could be contributing to the problems in your relationship. The following tips will assist you in transitioning to an easier and more secure attachment style:

Improve your non-verbal communication skills

When you interact with people, you constantly give and receive non-verbal signals through the gestures you use, your posture, and other similar signals. These non-verbal signals send powerful messages about what you truly feel. Learning to understand, read and communicate non-verbally will help you improve and strengthen your bonds with people. In addition, it is possible to develop these abilities by staying in the present, coping with anxiety, and enhancing your awareness of emotions.

Boost your emotional intelligence

Emotional intelligence, also known as emotional quotient or EQ, is the ability to recognize and use your emotions positively. This allows you to empathize more effectively with your spouse and to handle conflict more positively. Alongside helping increase your reading ability and communicating non-verbally, developing emotional intelligence can strengthen your relationship with your partner. When you understand and learn to manage your emotions, you will be able to communicate your desires and emotions to your loved one and also be able to discern what your partner feels.

Build relationships with secure people

A relationship with someone with an insecure attachment style can lead to a relationship that is not in sync, confusing, rocky, or even impossible. While you might be able to overcome your anxiety as a couple, you might want to find someone who can help you move beyond negative thinking and behaviors. A positive and supportive relationship with someone who makes you feel appreciated is crucial in establishing a feeling of security. Research indicates that between 50 and 60% of people have a secure attachment type, and insecure people therefore have a great chance of finding an intimate partner to help them overcome their fears. Forming strong bonds with these people can aid in recognizing and implementing new behavior patterns.

Resolve any childhood trauma

As we have discussed, trauma as an infant or young child can affect the bonding process. Trauma can occur in childhood from a dangerous or unstable environment, losing your primary caregiver, serious health problems, neglect, or abuse. Fear and despair can persist in adulthood if childhood trauma is not addressed.

Even if the trauma occurred several years ago, there are steps you can follow to get over the hurt, restore your emotional equilibrium, gain confidence, and reconnect in relationships.

5.4. Insecure Attachment and Psychopathology

In a framework of developmental psychopathology, attachment theory holds the possibility of explaining the emergence of psychopathology. Secure attachment does not cause psychopathology directly; however, the early childhood connection, the familial context, and other experiences with social connections can influence a person's behavior so that certain development patterns will be more likely over others. Evidence suggests a strong connection between insecure attachment and depression in young children, teens and adults. In addition, with self-report measures, the association between depression and insecure attachment is not proven to be a result of the current state of mood. The data also indicate that an insecure relationship is linked with adolescent anxiety-related symptoms. Thus the insecure dimensions of attachment could be a risk factor for depressive and anxiety indicators.

Insecure attachment can cause cognitive vulnerability to depression, particularly problematic attitudes. Attachment dynamics influence individuals' schemas and beliefs about others and the perceptions of cognitive events in the world. Bowlby (1980) declared that people create mental models that incorporate representations of themselves and others through interactions with their caregivers and other significant people. These internal working models are believed to form the foundation for one's thoughts, behavior, emotions, and feelings concerning the future relationship. Analyzing these models can help us understand the pathways to development that can lead to the symptoms of anxiety and depression, perhaps through the vulnerability of cognitive processes.

Bowlby's working models, which are thought to be within the context of the infant/caregiver relationship, are similar to the vulnerability in cognitive functioning Beck described in his theory about depression's cognitive aspects. Beck (1987) believed that schemas are what filter and affect information. Schemas are the result of dysfunctional attitudes, which are cognitive outcomes. Numerous studies have shown that dysfunctional attitudes can lead to depression in young adults and anxiety in adults.

Evidence and theory also show a link between insecure attachment and dysfunctional attitudes. So far, only a handful of studies have revealed that an insecure attachment can be related to dysfunctional attitudes and depression in adults. Research discovered that attachment was linked to low self-esteem, dysfunctional attitudes, and a negative attributional style within the sample of adolescents. Attachment was studied as a factor in the connection between cognitive style and parenting; however, depressive symptoms were not identified as an outcome. According to our research, no research has examined the relationship between insecure attachment, dysfunctional attitudes, and symptoms of depression among adolescents. Due to the rise in depression during adolescence, it is essential to examine whether the suggested pathway of cognitive influences that mediate the relationship between insecure attachment and depression symptoms applies to adolescents. Concerning anxiety, just one study has looked at the relationship between dysfunctional attitudes, insecure attachment, or anxieties. However, other studies have observed that anxiety is connected to hyper-vigilance and anxiety.

A person's dysfunctional attitude towards their self-image is believed to impact self-esteem, a more accessible and proximal indicator of emotional anxiety. Low self-esteem and a dysfunctional attitude are believed to cause the relationship between insecure attachment and subsequent depression, and research on adults supports this theory. The insecure attachment was linked to negative attitudes that resulted in lower self-esteem, and low self-esteem is associated with more depression symptoms. According to our research, no research has looked into this developmental process of mediation in adolescents. None of the studies that have examined this pathway to predict anxiety were discovered.

While there is evidence to support this mediatory pathway to predict symptoms of depression theoretically, it is plausible to conclude that this could also be a factor in anxiety-related symptoms, particularly since anxiety and depression symptoms frequently co-exist. Because the majority of studies that have investigated this pathway have been focused exclusively on symptoms of depression, this book will incorporate anxiety. As a result, to investigate whether avoidance and anxious attachments differ in their ability to predict anxiety and depressive symptoms related to the tri-dimensional model of depression and anxiety.

5.5. How to Overcome Insecure Attachment

Certain psychologists, like John Bowlby, consider that how an individual is attached cannot be changed. When a person reaches adulthood, they will remain in the grip of their personality and attachment style, which will influence their relationships with others. Nevertheless, recent research on attachment theory has shown that there are methods to manage and even overcome anxiety-inducing attachment. One method is the utilization of psychotherapy. Different kinds of psychotherapy could be beneficial, for instance, Cognitive Behavioral Therapy (CBT), which focuses on and challenges the distortions of thinking and negative behaviors.

Different psychodynamic psychotherapies, including therapy focused on transference, have been proven to aid patients in understanding and working on aspects of troublesome relationships. In addition, psychotherapy can assist in uncovering particular childhood traumas and experiences that have shaped adult attachment patterns and empower individuals to transform these unconsciously influenced influences. Couples and group therapy could also prove beneficial. Other methods to overcome insecure attachments are:

- Secure attachment learning as an adult: In order to build secure connections at an adult age, one may change how they see intimacy and relationships.

- Other types of psychotherapy: Psychotherapy can assist in identifying some of the traumas and behavior patterns that lead to negative thinking found throughout adulthood. If people access the root cause of their emotions, they will have greater control over their behavior.

Insecure attachment types can cause problems in intimate relationships. However, it is possible to overcome them by being open, determined, dedicated, and supportive of others.

5.5.1. Insecure Attachment Is Not Your Fault

Perhaps you have a relationship where your spouse is loving one day and distant the next. Perhaps you were in a relationship with someone who constantly checked in on you, demanded confirmation of their love, and maybe even distrusted you to have your privacy. Maybe you were the one who was insecure. If so, have you ever wondered why you are not able to feel confident in a loving relationship even though you work hard not to overburden your spouse? Or why you cannot avoid feeling warm and cold at times and hesitant to commit, but also want to be connected?

It is not because you chose the dramatic route, are unwilling to make a decision, or are emotionally clingy. The way you connect is something that you generally "inherit," not something you pick. You are likely to have this type of attachment without realizing it exists.

People who exhibit an anxious or avoidant attachment style do not have to suffer the negative effects of it for the rest of their lives. Let us discuss ways you can conquer an insecure attachment style.

5.6. What Should You Do If Your Attachments Are Not Secure?

Find a partner with a secure attachment style.

One of the most effective methods to "learn" secure attachment is to witness it in action and experience how wonderful it feels. This is why it is so important to have a spouse who is secure in their attachment and who is emotionally open and willing to be supportive of you. What can you do to determine if a potential partner has a secure attachment style?

Let your emotions be known.

- Provide and be willing to receive emotional help.

- Be independent, but be ready to share your feelings.

Conversely, the red flags of an insecure attachment method are:

- They want to closely monitor you.

- They need constant assurance of your love.

- They are hesitant to touch or get emotionally intimate.

A secure partner can be a role model of how to feel secure and open to emotions. In addition, it provides you with a safe space to experiment with the concept of secure bonding on your own. Be patient and express your gratitude to your partner often. You both deserve credit for the hard work you put into this!

Practice intimacy

If you have an insecure attachment type, you are likely to struggle with closeness or commitment. Perhaps you resent yourself for letting go of a loving relationship since you could not move on to the next stage. How do you get over the fear that is built in? The simple answer is to do the practice. In the case of emotional intimacy, you can try it out by deliberately approaching it with your partner. Consider this method similar to exposure therapy. It is a highly effective approach to behavioral therapy for those suffering from various phobias. For example, if someone is suffering from a serious fear of spiders, exposure therapy could involve intently watching spiders, being close to, or engaging in play with the spiders. The theory is that avoiding spiders will only increase fear. However, if you do encounter them, it will prove that they are not all bad. They allow your body and brain to become accustomed to spiders so you will not be scared.

If you are looking to develop emotional intimacy, practice by consciously addressing it with your partner. Ask each other questions like:

- If you could choose anyone on earth, who would you like to be your dinner guests?

- Are you aware of a nefarious thought about how you will pass away?

- What is your most precious memory?

- Have you ever cried in front of someone else? On your own?

Researchers found that people felt more connected to each other when they asked strangers to sit in a room together and engage in conversation using these prompts. Some even fell in love! Many couples saw the amazing results of this study when it was featured in a *New York Times* Modern Love article. It is worth a try.

Be patient, but focus on emotional regulation and interpersonal effectiveness.

Even if you find an emotionally secure partner, you probably will not change your relationship style overnight. So keep your eyes on the prize and let your experience serve as your guide. Be aware of when things do not go as planned and be willing to accept responsibility for your part. A study has shown that even in unstable relationships, the capacity to manage their emotions helped people avoid difficulties with intimacy. Doing your best to improve yourself will benefit you. To enhance your emotional control and other relationship skills, seek outside assistance. Therapy with an impartial and experienced expert can assist you in recognizing patterns in your relationships and reviewing situations that you may have misinterpreted. Set goals for how to behave differently. A dialectical behavior therapy (DBT) therapist can teach you specific techniques to manage emotions and resolve conflicts. They could teach you how to:

- Face an emotional "hot moment" by slowing down and stop performing or speaking in a way that causes harm

- Look at the evidence versus your assumptions

- Express your feelings in a genuine, honest, gentle, and respectful manner to your partner.

Psychology Today can help you find a therapist specializing in DBT or other relationship-related issues. These tools will help you be more aware of your relationships and develop trust, communication, and support for those most important to you.

5.6.1. Does It Make Sense for Adults to Modify An Insecure Attachment Style?

What can you do if you notice the signs of one of these attachment styles in yourself or someone you love? The trick is acknowledging that the switch for emotional intimacy needs to be turned on. It can be a challenge and requires an enormous amount of work.

- What does it feel like? The insecure adult must pay close attention to the physical and emotional sensations triggered by (emotional) intimate relationships. Self-reflection can help you understand and analyze the patterns already in place.

- What is the most important thing I need? Another essential step is understanding, exploring, and emotionally communicating your needs.

- What can I do? At some point, the insecure adult may be able to build relations with other people. For example, they could take a step-by-step method of letting others in or responding to the emotional demands of their close family members.

Let us say you identify yourself as one of the "insecure" adult attachment types. Maybe you are too emotionally distant or overly concerned about being close to those you love. Whatever the situation, it can aid you in coming to terms with how you interact with others. To manage your current attachment pattern, it is possible to comprehend your life as a unified narrative that has brought you from one set of experiences to another and contributed to shaping the person you are today. Psychotherapy could assist in achieving this. Like everything else, you may have to analyze your relationship patterns to better understand yourself. Nevertheless, should you choose to do so, take the time to do so, and avoid self-criticism.

Final Words About Insecure Attachment

Finding security after years of insecure attachment patterns can be challenging. Nevertheless, although it is a risk, it may be a source of security and the love you have always desired. A secure, earned attachment style could forever alter your life and relationships for the better.

Chapter 6

AVOIDANT ATTACHMENT

6.1. What Does Avoidant Attachment Mean?

Avoidant attachment is a form of attachment that a child develops when their primary caretaker is not showing care or concern for their needs like shelter and food. The child ignores their own issues and needs to keep the peace and ensure their caregiver is near. As a result, they struggle and experience sadness or anxiety. This attachment pattern typically occurs into and throughout adulthood and can impact relationships with their loved ones, friends, and other relationships. About 30% of people nowadays exhibit an avoidant attachment pattern.

Avoidant attachment is just one of four types of attachment that are developed in early childhood. Avoidant attachment is when a child or an infant does not receive the love and attention they need to build an enduring relationship with their caregiver or parent. An avoidant attachment style can result in a child hiding their emotions and being emotionally detached from their parents or caregivers. Nevertheless, the child wants to be close to the other person and may experience anxiety when they are separated. Avoidant adults may be unable to form close relationships because of their independence and unable to rely on other people for help or support. If you are worried your child may suffer from avoidant attachment issues, consult a therapist or doctor.

6.1.1. Causes of Avoidant Attachment

An avoidant attachment style can be created by the following caregiver behaviors:

- Being unresponsive when a baby or child is crying

- Actively preventing crying

- In no way displaying emotional reactions to issues or accomplishments

- Making fun of children's difficulties

- Acting displeased with a child who has an issue

- Not taking care of nutritional or medical needs

- Avoiding physical contact.

Children also may develop avoidant attachment behaviors because of adoption or their parents' illnesses, divorce, death, or divorce.

6.1.2. Signs of Avoidant Attachment

Anyone with avoidant attachment patterns might exhibit signs of anxiety and depression. In addition, children with avoidant parents or caregivers may not publicly show a desire for love or affection.

They are likely to:

- Avoid contact with your body

- Avoid eye contact

- Never or seldom solicit help

- Consume food in bizarre or unorthodox ways.

When children who have avoidant attachment mature and develop, they might show signs of it in their interactions and behavior, such as:

- Problems expressing or feeling emotions

- Feeling uncomfortable with physical proximity and touching

- Accusing partner of being too attached or too connected

- Refusing emotional or help from other people

- Believing that getting close to a partner could hurt them

- Craving a sense of independence and freedom at the expense of the partnership

- Refraining from relying on their partner in stressful times or allowing the partner to count on them

- Appearing cool and calm in high-energy circumstances.

6.1.3. The Signs of Avoidant Attachment Styles in Adults

Adults who exhibit the dismissive or avoidant attachment type generally appear to be pretty content with their actions and who they are. They could be extremely friendly, relaxed, and fun to spend time with. In addition, they may have lots of acquaintances or lovers. Therefore, they are generally not lonely or alone. Adults who avoid are generally self-sufficient. As a result, their self-esteem is very high, and they do not count on others to provide reassurance or emotional help. These individuals may invest in their professional growth and their confidence will increase with each achievement.

6.2. How Do Children Form an Avoidant Attachment Style?

The growth of an avoidant attachment style in children is largely due to the emotional presence of the caregivers. The caregivers do not necessarily leave the child alone. Nevertheless, they may avoid showing emotions and affection and are usually not emotionally attuned to the child's needs. They are also insecure and tend to back off when a child reaches out for help, encouragement, and love. The caregivers will likely get less attentive when the situation becomes emotionally intense. They could be overwhelmed and desire to get away. Their inability to be available is most apparent.

The child expresses a desire for intimacy, but they do not receive it. As a result, they may become withdrawn may be unable to express their emotions. Parents may also disapprove of and even reject any empathetic display of their child regardless of whether the emotion is negative (sadness or worry) or positive (excitement or joy). If a display of emotion is observed, parents can get angry and attempt to alter their child's actions by encouraging the child to grow up. Parents expect their young children to behave in a manner that is independent, calm, and cautious. Being raised in this environment can lead to an avoidant attachment style. The majority of caregivers who raise such children are affected by this style of attachment themselves. Because the parent was raised this way, they can pass the attachment pattern on to their children without being aware of it.

Why do some parents who are conscious of wanting to provide the most for their child struggle to stay connected or be emotionally attached to their child? Researchers have identified various factors. When they studied a variety of emotionally distant moms, researchers discovered that their inability to communicate with their children was likely due to their ignorance of "how to support others." A few mothers had a lack of empathy, while others were unable to create a sense of intimacy and dedication. Many had a childhood history of negative attachment experiences hence the limited repertoire of caregiving strategies at their disposal.

It is interesting to note that a recent review of research into attachment offered additional evidence for the intergenerational transmission of attachment style; it also revealed important connections between parents' avoidant ways of caring for their children as well as their child's avoidant bond, particularly among older adolescents and children.

6.3. What Kinds Of Behaviors Are Connected with Avoidant Attachment Among Children?

Many toddlers who avoid their parents are self-contained, quick-witted "little adults" and can be expected to behave as such. Avoidant attachment sufferers are taught to avoid expressing a desire for affection, warmth, or closeness. However, on an emotional level, they show the same degree of reaction and the same amount of anxiety as children who are not. Children who are easily attached are inclined to seek closeness to their loved ones but cannot interact or relate to them.

6.3.1. Avoidant Adult Relationships

Relationships and bonds are generally shallow for adults who are not social. For a meaningful interaction and rewarding, it must become deeper. Avoidant adults generally avoid intense displays of intimacy and closeness. They tend to shut themselves off when things become serious. At this point, they may look for an excuse to end their relationship. They may become extremely annoyed by their partner's actions, habits, or physical appearance. Ultimately, they begin drifting away and separating themselves from their partner. Adults with this type of attachment think they do not require an emotional connection in their lives. This is the direct result of their upbringing. The caregivers they had taught them that they could not be relied upon. When they needed emotional support, it was not given. As a result, they no longer look for it from others. It is like they have turned off the switch.

6.4. The Dismissive Attachment Style in Adults

A dismissive attachment is a relationship that has a strong connection with one's parents. People tend to avoid emotional intimacy because they have learned to separate themselves from their needs early in life and reduce their emotions' importance.

Disengaged adults will be more attracted to close relationships and enjoy spending time with their partners. However, they may feel uncomfortable if their relationship gets too intimate. To deal with their emotions, they resort to repression to hide their vulnerability. Indirect methods include complaining, sulking, or sneering if they need support from their partner.

Research by Fraley and Brumbaugh shows that most disengaged adults use "pre-emptive strategies" to disable the attachment system. For example, they might decide not to get involved in a relationship with someone they love out of fear of rejection. They may avoid undesirable sights or "tune out" when discussing attachment issues. They can also choose to "bury" memories that are not favorable, such as a break-up.

People with this attachment type tend to focus on themselves and their lifestyle and tend to ignore the interests and feelings of others. They also have difficulty sharing their thoughts and feelings with their loved ones. Their usual response to disputes, conflicts, or other stressful situations is to remain distant. Disengaged adults tend to be optimistic about themselves and negatively view others. This self-esteem boost protects the fragile self, which is vulnerable to rejection and insults. This is often a result of low self-esteem or feelings of self-resentment. Avoidant partners often react with anger to perceived insults or challenges to their self-esteem.

To the avoidant adult, emotional intimacy and closeness are not often on the agenda. On the outside, a person with an avoidant attachment style could appear strong and confident. However, this does not necessarily mean they are not experiencing pain or making the people around them suffer. The inability to create a strong, lasting, and meaningful relationship can be a painful experience for people who have this type of attachment. In addition, it can be devastating their loved ones. Additionally, the fact that you have an avoidant attachment style as a parent is more likely to influence your child's bonding style. You will probably transmit it to your child if you suffer from it.

6.4.1. Can Adults Alter Their Style of Attachment?

Therapy could be the best approach to creating a secure attachment. However, if this is not the best option, you could also consider online classes. If you want to change, you must make an effort. It does not matter if you are working through it with a trusted partner, a therapist, or even a textbook; regularity and determination are the most important factors.

6.4.2. Life with Avoidant Attachment

Avoidant attachers tend to keep their private lives secret and avoid emotionally challenging discussions. They are susceptible to shutting down, becoming numb, rigid compartmentalizing, and pushing others away.

However, there is a distinction between someone who is an absolutely rude person and someone with a tendency to avoid attachment. Suppose unacceptable behaviors from your partner irritate your nervous system or seem like alarms. In that case, this is an appropriate reason to break off the relationship! Do not remain in relationships that are unhealthy.

6.5. Negative Thoughts

Negative thoughts and inner voices can further magnify the distrustful, and negative attitudes avoidants have towards other people. Conversely, people who avoid others often have positive, friendly views of themselves. These views can be used to cover up self-degrading or self-destructive thoughts. Both voices are part of an internal model that works based on the person's first attachments. These serve as a guideline for interacting with your loved partner. A critical voice may be viewed as the filter through which people examine themselves, their partners, and relationships generally. Though many critical inner voices are not fully aware, they can determine how people react to one another in their most intimate and close relationships.

6.6. How Do We convert an Avoidant Attachment to a Secure One?

We do not need to live with the attachment defense strategies we learned early in our lives. Many experiences in life offer opportunities for personal growth, transformation, and learning.

Although your attachment patterns are set in your childhood and continue throughout your life, you can create a secure attachment at any age. This is best achieved by making sense of your story. Attachment research shows that the best way to predict a child's attachment security is not how his parents raised him as a child but how they made sense of his childhood experiences. To "make sense" of your life experiences, the first step is to organize a narrative that will help to understand how your childhood experiences have impacted your present. You can reprogram your brain to have more confidence in yourself and your relationships if you create a cohesive story.

Therapy is another way to make changes. Therapy alliances provide a safe environment for us to examine our attachment histories and gain new perspectives about ourselves, other people, and relationships. If you are someone who exhibits a dismissive-avoidant attachment style, it does not mean that you are damaged in some way. Instead, it indicates your needs were not addressed correctly in your childhood, leading to your self-sufficiency. If you want to change how you connect with others, you can make it happen, and more meaningful connections and relationships may be on the horizon.

6.7. Treatments for Avoidant Attachment

Avoidant attachments can hinder healthy and fulfilling relationships between people and their families, partners, and friends. However, it is possible to change from avoidant attachment to secure one by undergoing therapy. Cognitive behavior therapy (CBT) helps identify harmful thought patterns and behavior, determine why and how they manifest, and then reverse them using play, problem-solving, and developing confidence in yourself. For example, CBT can help address negative beliefs and thoughts and develop secure attachment thoughts in their place to prevent avoidant attachment. The right therapy is the most important aspect of treating avoidant attachment. You must feel at ease with your therapist and be confident enough to count on them. In the therapy process, consistency is essential even if you believe that your thinking and behavior are changing quickly.

6.8. Preventing Avoidant Attachment in Children

As parents, you can assist your child in developing an attachment that is secure:

- Be mindful of your emotional state and how you express it to your child.

- Insist on getting enough sleep. Making time for sleep when you are a parent can be challenging; however, a lack of sleep can cause you to be more stressed and less capable of managing your emotions. Get your spouse, your relatives, and friends to assist with chores and other responsibilities to ensure you have the time you need to have a restful night's sleep.

- Be attentive to your child's facial expressions, sounds, and movements in different scenarios. For instance, your baby's crying could sound different when hungry than when they are exhausted.

- Spend time with your child. Play with them and talk to them. Play peek-a-boo with them, hug them, smile at them, and let them know that you want to spend time with them.

Do not place too much pressure on yourself to be the "perfect" parent. Each individual interaction is not going to determine the way your child connects. Instead, connecting to your children and trying your best to be accessible to them will help you get on the right path toward creating healthy attachment patterns.

Chapter 7

FEARFUL AVOIDANT ATTACHMENT

A person is said to have fearful-avoidant attachment when they crave a relationship but simultaneously wish to avoid having one. In this chapter, we will examine not just the definition of the term "fearful-avoidant attachment" but also its symptoms and the available treatments for those who suffer from this condition.

7.1 What is Fearful Avoidant Attachment?

A fearful-avoidant attachment style is a form of adult attachment characterized by the need to protect oneself and avoid relationships and the simultaneous desire to remain in one. A fearful-avoidant attachment style is also characterized by an inclination to avoid situations where a person fears they may get hurt.

People with fearful-avoidant attachment disorder have a poor view of themselves and the people in their immediate surroundings. They may feel, for instance, that they do not deserve to be loved or that others should not be loved or trusted due to their propensity to betray or reject them. People with fearful-avoidant attachment styles have a propensity to have poor self-esteem. Consequently, they tend to seek validation from others in the hopes that it will make them feel better about themselves. As a result, there is a greater dependence on other individuals and a drive to gain their approval.

Individuals with fearful attachment styles are pessimistic about themselves and unable to form meaningful relationships with others. Fearful attachments are often associated with traumatic experiences that occurred during childhood and have a tendency to cause more unfavorable consequences than the other three attachment types. Adults who battle with this anxiety are more prone to have pessimistic views of both themselves and the world. They are very reliant on the acceptance and affirmation of others' thoughts. They have high anxiety levels and a great yearning for intimacy, yet they avoid intimate relationships out of fear of being disappointed or rejected. Despite their elevated anxiety levels, they have a strong yearning for closeness.

7.2 The Causes of Fearful Attachment

The fearful attachment style is a subtype of insecure attachment that may be subdivided further (along with anxious and avoidant). According to Maggie Holland, MA, MHP, and LMHC, most children develop insecure attachment patterns throughout early childhood. Nevertheless, it is not impossible for the experiences you encounter as an adult to impact your attachment style. Those with fearful-avoidant attachment styles were often trained to be very autonomous as youngsters, to the point where they think that relationships are unnecessary or unsafe. This likely contributed to their development of an attachment style characterized by aversion to intimate attachments. It is possible that parents or guardians were very rigid or indifferent to their children's emotions and need for physical contact. In other words, if a child's mental and physical requirements were not addressed during their formative years, they were unable to rely on the connections in their lives.

Significant life events that leave you with a sense of isolation or abandonment, such as seeing your parents struggle through a nasty divorce, can also alter your relationships with other people.

7.3 The Factors Contributing to Fearful Avoidance

Even though it is difficult to generalize about this attribute, people with fearful avoidant attachment styles often strongly dislike the possibility of rejection. People are, by nature, social creatures who need interaction with others. Those with fearful attachments, however, learned as children that they could not rely on these connections when they needed aid. They often believe their desires are unworthy of being fulfilled and that others will let them down. As a result, people often retreat from social interaction in an attempt to avoid rejection.

According to Silvi Saxena, MBA, MSW, LSW, CCTP, OSW-C, persons who are afraid and avoidant have a history of broken attachments. This is generally the result of neglectful childhood circumstances or any tumultuous relationship. Saxena has an array of professional credentials and a broad experience in social work. They fear loneliness yet are hesitant to establish meaningful relationships with others. As a result, those who are fearful-avoidant often have a history of severed bonds.

7.4 Desires in the Fearful-Avoidant Attachment

Dr. Krista Jordan, Ph.D., a Texas-based psychotherapist, argues; "Those with a fearful attachment style have the same fundamental desires that all humans have." This desire is to develop strong relationships that offer a sense of protection and security. Those with fearful-avoidant attachment have learned that having desires and goals that involve other people will always end in being disregarded, forgotten, and rejected. Nonetheless, they wish to find happiness in solid, healthy relationships with friends and a love partner(s). When a connection grows too intimate, a person may perceive that they are in danger. That does not mean they do not want them; it simply means they have been taught that relationships may be a cause of sadness.

7.5 Fearful Attachment in Adults

In adults, fearful attachment manifests predominantly via the relationship dynamic. According to Jordan, a fearful infant might make a feeble attempt to approach a parent before abruptly stopping and collapsing in sheer terror. The youngster may, after that, scream in agony. A terrified adult, however, may phone you and set up a date, only to cancel at the last minute due to an awful sense of dread. This may be because their dread is too great for them to bear.

Such individuals may feel so overcome by the conflict between their opposing desires for connection and safety that they think the best course of action is to spend more time alone. Adults with a fearful attachment style may see themselves as unworthy of affection, appreciation, or connection. As infants, they faced a pattern of approaching their caregivers with a need, but the caretaker failed to respond and provide that need. This pattern remained constant throughout their growth. This may seem little to us as adults, but from the viewpoint of a child, this is virtually a complete rejection.

Adults with a fearful attachment will frequently get close to another person before withdrawing from the connection to avoid the rejection they anticipate. This is the brain's way of protecting itself since it has learned that connection is potentially dangerous.

7.6 Loving Someone with a Fearful Attachment Style

If you are in a relationship with someone who has a fearful attachment type, the following recommendations, which have been approved by experts, may help:

7.6.1 Convince and emphasize that you are a reliable source by providing evidence of your credibility.

The most crucial thing you can do is to guarantee that your communication with your spouse is clear and straightforward and that you only say what you mean. Please do not make a promise unless you are confident you will be able to keep it. Patience is necessary since your partner must repeatedly see that you will always show up for them.

7.6.2 Encourage them to replace their negative inner monologue with a new story

Individuals with fearful attachment styles often entertain negative thoughts about themselves. You may help people unlearn these behaviors by subtly reminding them, over time, of their already impressive traits.

7.6.3 Do not let the actions of others influence how you feel about yourself

Realize that this is not your partner's reaction to you, but rather to relationships in general. Your spouse may have been participating in these behaviors long before you met them. Remembering this might save you from feeling injured when their profound ambivalence arises.

7.6.4 Be ready for a non-linear sequence of occurrences

Your spouse may make some progress but then regress; if this occurs, you should be patient and soothing. Establishing trust is very important, and in order to do it, you must be completely open, reliable, and honest. Because they are programmed to see others as potential dangers, it may be more challenging to convince themselves that you are a trustworthy individual.

7.6.5 Recognize that the number of things you can do is limited

To love someone with a fearful attachment type is to support them in recognizing and respecting the fundamental issues they face and, if necessary, to encourage them to seek the assistance of a qualified expert. The most important thing is to be there for them and provide support as they go along their road to better comprehend who they are.

7.7 Fearful avoidant attachment handling in breakups

People in this kind of relationship have an unhealed wound from previous instances of abandonment, and breakups may be pretty traumatic for them. Even the most emotionally "healed" person may have a negative response. The vast majority of the time, the individual with a fearful-avoidant attachment type will initiate the breakup. This is typically an effort to shield themselves from what they perceive as inevitable. They might experience regret and sorrow if they cared about you, but they would ultimately see it as a necessary pain.

When they are not the ones who initiated the breakup, it just helps to reinforce their past fears of their relationships ending in rejection. Withdrawal, feelings of despair, and frequent, painful conversations with oneself are all possible outcomes. Fearful avoidants have difficulty breaking up with a partner and preventing a breakup from diminishing their sense of self-worth. Those who struggle articulating their emotions may find breaking up with a lover particularly difficult. Fearful-avoidant attachment folks may likely believe they "deserved" the breakup and that it was inevitable, and they are unlikely to follow up with inquiries or attempt to rekindle the relationship.

They may feel depressed one day, emotionally aloof and alienated the next. These individuals are driven by two competing forces inside themselves: one of these forces desires and demands connection. At the same time, the other is profoundly mistrustful and scared of it. The part of them that fears connection will be relieved that they no longer need to worry about it, while the part of them that craves connection will be distressed by the separation.

7.8 Communicating with a Fearful-Avoidant Person

Communication is the cornerstone of every happy and healthy relationship, but when one partner has an insecure attachment style, the significance of communication increases exponentially. By adhering to these standards, it is possible to have conversations that are not only helpful but also thought-provoking.

7.8.1 Ensure that there are always open channels of communicatio

Communicate like you would (ideally) with all of your other relationships. Be forthright, straightforward, and honest, and do what you say you will do. Due to their underlying fear, it may be challenging to communicate with someone with this attachment type. If there is any uncertainty, ask your partner for clarity, and encourage them to do the same. This will guarantee that you and your spouse have the same vision for your relationship's future.

7.8.2 Have them read positive statements to themselves

By expressing compassion and empathy, you may demonstrate that you care about them and can connect to what they are experiencing. According to Jordan, you should let them know that you want to be there for them and recognize that it may be difficult for them to fully commit to relationships. Expect that they may have histories of abuse or neglect, and help them to feel comfortable discussing childhood memories by presenting them as resilient persons who overcame adversity (rather than victims). This will make them more at ease when discussing their childhood memories. Maintain an open mind and be willing to accompany them to couples therapy while they seek to improve their relationship skills.

7.8.3 Examine your typical modes of communication

Due to their heightened sensitivity to risks to their safety, you should avoid raising your voice, breaking objects, making emotional or physical threats, or otherwise making them uncomfortable. Even in the middle of a dispute, it may be beneficial to demonstrate that you are not a threat by adopting a softer voice, a friendlier tone, or even just an odd grin. Sometimes even expressive hand gestures can make a person with a history of traumatic events feel uneasy. Therefore, you must remain open to the notion that your unconscious communication practices may contribute to their fear. Due to this, you should be willing to examine your unconscious communication patterns, which may be contributing to their dread. Consider the likelihood that they see relationships through the prism of a painful history. Remember this while you deal with them. When someone discusses something with you, display active listening skills and confirm what they are saying without adding your personal tales or experiences.

7.9 Dealing with a Fearful-Avoidant Attachment Style

7.9.1 Gain an understanding of the kind of relationship you value

It may be beneficial to educate yourself on the topic of attachment and determine what attachment type you believes you possess. Then, consider your behavior in your current relationships and with the adults responsible for your care when you were a youngster, and make conclusions based on both sets of experiences. Determining how to begin working with an insecure attachment may be facilitated by first acquiring knowledge of your attachment type.

7.9.2 Self-Awareness

It would help if you attempted to identify the triggers for your fearful-avoidant behavior. This will assist you in dealing with similar circumstances more successfully. Be cognizant of this fact if anytime you see a little difference in your partner's behavior, the first idea that enters your mind is that they are cheating on you or turning their back on you. Consider why you have these sentiments and what a more hopeful way of thinking might be. Consider the possibility that if you see a shift in your partner's body language, they are tired from having had a terrible day, rather than automatically assuming that they are concealing anything from you. If you are conscious of the thoughts that go through your mind and make an effort to question them when they appear, you may be able to respond in a manner that is more beneficial to your mental and physical health.

7.9.3 Develop your interpersonal communication skills

Develop the practice of communicating in a way that not only makes your desires understood but is healthy and prevents confrontation. Rather than assigning blame or passing judgment, express how you feel. You may do this by composing sentences that begin with the word "I," such as "I was irritated when you did X." As a result, your spouse will be less likely to feel attacked, and there will be fewer misconceptions about how you feel about the issue. Make a habit of communicating your expectations in a manner that is both courteous and clear and plain. For example, you may say something like, "I need to feel encouraged while I accomplish X" or "I need some time alone to carry out X." These assertions are true. Each of these two propositions is true in its manner. Instead of making indirect efforts to drive your spouse away, it will be much simpler for them to comprehend what you are searching for from them.

7.9.4 Consider enrolling in therapy

If you believe you need more assistance regulating your attachment pattern or want to learn how to become more secure, you may consider attending counseling. Participating in therapy may help you discover the patterns of your attachments, analyze your thoughts about yourself, and develop healthy approaches to your relationships with others. All these things are achievable if you are prepared to do the necessary work. Cognitive behavioral therapy, or CBT, is a talk therapy that aims to aid patients in recognizing and challenging detrimental patterns of thought, emotion, and behavior. Interpersonal therapy is a specialized kind of psychotherapy that teaches patients how to improve their relationships with the people in their immediate surroundings and with members of other social groupings. This may be advantageous for someone who desires to modify their attachment style and become more secure in their relationships. In addition, psychodynamic psychotherapy may aid persons with a fearful-avoidant attachment in understanding how their attachment style affects their adult relationships.

7.10 How Does a Fearful-Avoidant Attachment Affect the Relationship?

People who struggle with a fearful attachment style have a poor self-image and a negative model of others; consequently, they fear intimacy and autonomy in their relationships. In addition, they are avoidant, socially reclusive, and mistrustful of others.

7.10.1 They find it challenging to commit to anything

A person with a fearful avoidant attachment style may find it difficult to commit to another person because they tend to avoid close relationships. They have a propensity for avoiding serious relationships while simultaneously searching for ways to connect with others and grow emotionally close to them. This is due to their inclination to avoid entering into committed relationships. The higher the intensity of their affections for one another, the more likely they are to engage in avoidance behavior. This tends to upset people and evokes sad memories of the past. When a couple decides to take their relationship to the next level, it is common for a fearful-avoidant partner to be scared. It is possible that they cannot fully believe that their spouse will always be there for them. This might be due to a fundamental lack of self-worth, a lack of confidence in others, or a mix of the two.

7.10.2 When they are near others, they experience discomfort

A person with a fearful-avoidant attachment style may find it difficult to commit to another person due to their deep-seated mistrust of others. This may impede their ability to build intimate connections. They often exhibit signals of a yearning for connection, yet they tend to push others away as the situation intensifies. When one approaches a fearful avoidant too closely, it may reawaken earlier wounds, and at this point, significant behavioral changes may be seen for the first time.

7.10.3 They like adopting a relaxed attitude to life

People with a fearful-avoidant attachment style are happiest when they maintain their interactions with romantic partners more informally. This is because they fear getting close to and trusting other people. They may be satisfied to continue in the dating stage of the relationship for a longer period since this stage meets their wants the best.

On the other hand, they may remain in platonic or noncommittal relationships not because they choose to but because they find the prospect of developing deeper feelings unpleasant. As a method to fulfill their want for attention without having to make long-term commitments, it is usual for individuals with this attachment style to seek out casual sexual experiences. This conduct is motivated by a desire to avoid a long-term obligation to any individual. According to findings reported by Favez and Tissot (2019), fearful avoidance is predictive of both a bigger number of sexual partners and a higher level of sexual compliance among men and women.

7.10.4 They maintain a psychological and physical separation between themselves and others

A person whose attachment style is defined by fear and avoidance may find comfort in maintaining a certain amount of emotional and physical space between themselves and their spouse. As a measure of self-protection, they may be hesitant to discuss important matters or offer an excessive quantity of personal information. If things get too complex for them or they are requested to reveal sensitive information, they may quickly become very mute.

7.10.5 They have an inaccurate conception of a relationship and how it should function

Since it is typical for persons with a fearful-avoidant attachment to have been raised in a chaotic environment, they likely assume this is how romantic relationships should be. If they are in a relationship with someone who radiates self-assurance and stays cool in difficult circumstances, they may develop a distrust for their partner. They may have a sneaky sense that something is amiss; consequently, they may create a dispute with their spouse or fabricate an issue to upset the relationship's status quo and make it less predictable.

7.10.6 They experience a larger degree of general sadness

A study examining the effect of attachment styles on romantic partnerships revealed that avoidant attachment styles were related to fewer instances of good emotions and more instances of negative feelings in romantic relationships.

7.10.7 They bring about their own failure

A person with a fearful avoidant attachment style may be more prone to harm a healthy love connection on their own out of fear that they are in danger. As a result, they tend to focus excessively on potential relationship difficulties, even when there is no need to be worried. They may accuse their spouse of wrongdoing or threaten to leave the relationship. As a result of each of these tactics, the other individual may begin to consider ending the relationship.

7.10.8 They are very sensitive

A person who is fearful avoidant may have heightened sensitivity to even the smallest changes in their partner's behavior. This might potentially strain their connection. Changes in body language, micro expressions, the tone of a person's voice, and lying are examples of potential triggers. A spouse who is fearful avoidant may accumulate knowledge about these seemingly little changes and conclude that their partner is concealing information, unfaithful, or engaging in some behavior that undermines trust. When this thought becomes ingrained in a person's mind, it enables them to strike out at their spouse or push them away in a manner they feel is protective, even if their partner has not participated in improper conduct. This enables them to distance themselves more from their lover.

PART 3 – HOW CAN I CHANGE MY ATTACHMENT STYLE?

Chapter 8

UNDERSTANDING MY TRIGGERS

Anxious attachment triggers are events, references, or social encounters that lead an already anxious individual to experience a significant increase in anxiety. What situations might trigger your anxiety and leave you powerless and despondent if you suffer from anxious attachment? When you are anxiously connected, almost anything might serve as a potential anxiety trigger. When you are desperately isolated, nearly nothing can reach you. However, as someone who suffered from worrying attachments for at least the first 21 years of my life, I can assure you that it does not need to be all-consuming. In actuality, the realization that everything has the potential to function as a trigger is what may genuinely free you from triggers, provided you respond correctly to them. However, this is only possible if you understand that everything has the potential to act as a trigger.

Developing the ability to regulate our thoughts, emotions, and behaviors is an essential skill to possess. Consider this one of the milestones to achieving your goal of building an "earned secure connection." Unfortunately, people prone to developing neurotic attachments may have difficulty getting acquainted with the concept of self-regulation. Every day, we all experience various happy and negative emotions of varying degrees, depending on their intensity, particularly in terms of one's capacity to build connections with others. Whether the relationship is strong and thriving or having minor difficulties, it is still possible to have emotional ups and downs. Occasionally, the journey is so incredible that you feel butterflies in your stomach. However, there are also times when your emotions may seem out of control, like you are on a roller coaster. Emotions can steer us correctly and assist us in making the most informed decisions possible throughout our lives. They are used as a compass. Occasionally, they may become so overwhelming that we act in destructive ways to ourselves and others when we seek to manage them.

This chapter will assist you in becoming aware of the typical triggers that affect individuals with an anxious attachment style. These triggers might vary from an individual's surroundings to his or her thoughts and emotions. In order to be prepared to control your responses to possible triggers, it is essential first to become aware of these potential triggers.

8.1 What is Self-Regulation?

Self-regulation is the capacity to manage one's emotions and behaviors that result directly from those emotions. Self-regulation may also refer to the capacity to regulate one's behavior. One must be able to self-regulate to sustain positive relationships, resolve conflicts effectively, and retain a continuous sense of self-confidence.

Few individuals are aware that our attachment style impacts our ability to manage our emotions and how we react to them. Therefore, it is necessary to have a thorough awareness of when it is acceptable to rely on our emotions. Nonetheless, it is also essential to be conscious of the occasions in which our attachment type influences our ability to self-regulate.

8.1.1 Secure Attachment Style

Even if you are in a committed relationship with another individual, this does not necessarily indicate that you have complete command over your emotions. However, those with a secure attachment style are generally sympathetic, sensitive to the feelings of others, and capable of creating appropriate limits for themselves and their relationships with others. As a result, persons with solid attachments are more likely to feel emotional stability and happiness in their relationships. In addition, they are confident in their ability to function both alone and in a relationship, allowing them to feel at ease in both contexts.

When presented with emotionally stimulating situations, a person with strong social ties may behave in the following six ways:

- They are candid about their genuine emotions with their closest friends and family members.

- They put into words the thoughts and feelings they are experiencing.

- They might try techniques such as meditation or therapy.

- They participate in physical activity to alleviate stress and boost endorphin levels.

- Even when they feel undesirable emotions, like wrath, they train themselves to be conscious of their thoughts.

- If they feel they might lose control of an emotionally charged situation, they remove themselves from it.

8.2 Anxious Attachment Style

An anxious attachment is characterized by constant anxiety over the dependability and safety of your intimate relationship. This anxiety manifests as a feeling of inadequacy in the relationship. If your principal caregivers did not reliably and consistently address your attachment requirements while you were young, you are more prone to develop anxious attachment, also known as preoccupied attachment. This is due to their inability to pay enough attention to you and earn your confidence. You may be unable to form good relationships with others as a result.

You may be somewhat surprised to find that anxious attachment has been prevalent in society since the start of the industrial revolution. This is due to interference with the human family unit and human tribal culture, which resulted in the partial collapse of both institutions. The following is a quotation from Robert Karen, Ph.D., the author of *Becoming Attached*:

Before the modern age, people favored spending most of their time with their families. Farmers, bakers, and cobblers would house hired laborers in their homes. If hired laborers were housed in the farmer's home, they would consider themselves members of the farmer's family. The respect shown to apprentices was equivalent to the respect accorded to sons. There were not that many people who woke up and went to work.

The environment may have been claustrophobic, with all of the rage, resentment, and murderous jealousies that usually arise in such situations, but there was also warmth, familiarity, and undeniable belonging. In contrast, contemporary society's focus on achievement, professions, and the conventional nuclear family has led to the formation of less-than-ideal settings for the development of newborns and children. A mother is probably unable to take a significant break from caring for her children and the rest of the family since she may be cut off from her relatives and friends.

We have no option but to admit that the overwhelming majority of persons who suffer from anxious attachment are the consequence of a general lack of emotional resources on the part of their parents and other principal caregivers. Not only has the former culture, which put a great value on children, been devalued, but many parents have been forced to detach from the enormous emotional demands their newborn places on them.

As a result, the whole society has been weakened. When raising their children, most parents do not have access to what may be described as "a village worth of extra hands." Isolation from other persons, not only the lack of emotionally available parents, is a crucial factor in the development of individuals with insecure attachment patterns.

8.2.1 What Variables Lead To The Formation of an Anxious Attachment in a Young Child?

People with an anxious attachment style may have had a caregiver who was not always reliable in addressing their needs as children. As a result, the youngster would be uncertain about what to anticipate from the caretaker. Would they be there for them when they needed support the most? Consequently, children learn to self-regulate by throwing temper tantrums, becoming inconsolable, and behaving very dependently. Behaving in this manner increases the likelihood that their caregiver will pay attention to them, allowing their anxious feelings to subside.

Individuals with an anxious attachment style may respond to emotionally stressful events in a variety of detrimental ways, such as:

- Constantly contemplating their relationship's dynamics

- Concentrating on the possible risks their relationship may face (whether they exist or not)

- Striving to get as emotionally and physically close to their spouse as possible

- Constantly attempting to communicate with their partner

- During a quarrel, they employ blame or guilt to persuade the other party to comply with one's desires.

- Having an outpouring of anger, mainly if some anger is directed within and towards oneself.

Adults with anxious attachments tend to obsess about possible risks to their relationships. Consequently, they are more prone to feel extreme wrath in reaction to these imagined threats.

As a consequence of their maladaptive approach to self-regulation, they may experience animosity towards their spouse, along with self-criticism, depression, and despair. A person with an anxious attachment style must learn how to self-regulate in order to build and sustain healthy relationships.

8.2.2 Self-Regulation Techniques for Anxious Attachment

To our great good fortune, acquiring control over our emotions is possible with a little effort and consistent practice. You may be able to improve your ability to self-regulate by participating in activities such as mindfulness, altering your way of thinking, and constructively managing your anger. Self-regulation is the capacity of a person to regulate their thoughts, emotions, and behaviors concerning their long-term goals. Before deciding on a plan of action, carefully study your available options. To do this, you must be aware of the elements that may work as triggers for you in your relationships.

When a person who struggles with anxious attachment experiences any of the following emotional triggers, it may create strain in their relationship:

- A spouse who does not maintain behavioral consistency

- When a spouse or partner forgets a momentous day,

such as a birthday or anniversary

- When your spouse gets home later than anticipated

- A spouse who does not respond to messages at regular intervals

- A spouse's inability to notice anything new (e.g., a new haircut).

When an adult with nervous attachment troubles attempts to rebuild a connection with their partner, each of these triggers may lead them to get excessively emotional and exacerbate the situation. This may be seen as an attempt to create a conflict or to get their partner's attention. These interpretations are both conceivable.

8.3 Twelve Anxious Attachment Triggers

A trigger is anything that has the potential to induce a particular emotion (and to amplify those feelings). People with attachment anxiety may find the following list of twelve potential triggers helpful:

- Attending a party to meet new people and increase one's social network.

- A buddy who is withdrawing from you.

- Your significant other has not called you in many days, and you are growing anxious.

- Your boyfriend or lover has been communicating with a third party.

- People make jokes about you that are not meant to be malicious and are done merely for amusement.

- Someone avoids you or otherwise sends rejection signals.

- People congregated in tight-knit clusters.

- Something that evokes negative memories.

- A significant examination.

- A competitive sport.

- Someone who reminds you of a childhood attachment figure who was the source of your grief.

- Being in the company of those who are too dedicated to their worries (two anxiously attached people spells problems).

Each of these components has the potential to trigger an event. Because the anxiously attached individual lives in an emotionally unpredictable environment daily, every part of their environment that heightens this sensation of unpredictability is a potential trigger for them. The mere fact that someone does not respond to your email or is not as emotionally or physically present for a short period is sufficient to cause doubt to build and increase.

8.3.1 Why Does Uncertainty Cause Anxious Attachment Triggers?

When you are anxiously attached, practically everything uncertain has the potential to serve as a trigger. This remains true even for circumstances that seem harmless. The lack of consistent support for developing appropriate emotional regulation abilities is the underlying cause of anxious attachment. As a result, even the slightest amount of uncertainty can operate as a trigger, and thus, even the smallest amount of ambiguity has the potential to produce anxious attachment. All moms of children with secure attachment exhibit the following set of good maternal characteristics and behaviors:

- Warmth

- Sensitivity

- Responsiveness

- Dependability

If your mother or father, or both, did not constantly display warmth, sensitivity, responsiveness, and dependability, you would not have had anybody to assist you in managing your emotions, coping with your stress, and feeling at ease in your surroundings. Consequently, your neurological system will develop differently from individuals with secure attachments, and this difference can be permanent. The inability to establish a connection with one's mother may lead to the development of an anxious attachment style since it teaches a person that experiencing emotions might put them in danger.

Consequently, almost anything that even somewhat approaches an element of uncertainty might trigger your anxiety. You are suppressing your emotions because you are attempting to exert more control over your surroundings and give the impression of being safe. This is the motivation for this behavior.

8.3.2 How Do I Manage Dating When I Have Anxious Attachment?

Due to their high stress, worry, and overthinking, individuals with an anxious attachments may find dating somewhat more challenging.

The ultimate objective is to establish a deeper connection with the person you are dating, regardless of whether that person is male or female. To date effectively, when you have an anxious attachment, you must take good care of yourself and recognize that you are vulnerable to getting harmed.

8.4. What Factors May Contribute to an Uncertain Attachment?

It is believed that individuals with anxious attachment did not have a secure and loving connection with their parents when they were younger and that this may be linked back to events that happened during infancy. This might result from emotional neglect, physical abuse, emotional desertion, inconsistent parenting, or a lack of focus on the child's needs. Even as an adult, a lack of a secure and loving relationship with one's parents may continue to have repercussions, especially on one's sexual relationships. This is particularly true if the absence of connection begins in infancy. As previously stated, a person with anxious attachment needs attention and continuous reassurance and often reports feeling excessively reliant in romantic relationships. In addition, they have an strong desire for consistent reassurance.

Given this, anything that makes them feel ignored or as like they are losing a loved one to another might be a trigger. For instance, if you and your significant other attend a party and your partner spends the whole evening talking to other guests, you may feel neglected and unhappy. You may experience a wide variety of negative emotions.

8.4.1 What are the origins of anxious attachment, and how is it treated?

When one considers the likelihood that anxious attachment may affect one's mental health, counseling is never a terrible option for a person struggling with this issue. Cognitive behavioral therapy, often abbreviated as CBT, is one of the various strategies that may be used to address a person's mental health issue. During this treatment style, the client works with a therapist to identify unhelpful habits and behaviors and develop problem-solving skills to manage their concerns better. In addition, the client tries to recognize patterns and behaviors potentially detrimental to their well-being.

Cognitive-behavioral therapy (CBT) may greatly assist if you have an anxious attachment style. This is due to CBT's emphasis on behavior rather than thought. You may find it beneficial to consult a therapist to identify the instances in which you feel the most neglected or need care and develop tactics for addressing these emotions in the future. An anxious attachment style will probably lead to difficulties in adult love relationships. Couples counseling may also help mitigate this issue's negative consequences and develop a healthier connection between the two parties involved.

Moreover, while we are on the subject of romantic relationships, one study indicated that appreciation from romantic partners was related to decreased levels of anxious attachment. Particularly if you do not already have a significant other, it is an excellent idea to hunt for someone exceptional at showing thankfulness. You and your significant other may choose to discuss the possibility of establishing a regular practice of gratitude together. Tell them exactly what they did to earn your thanks, and then request that they do the same for you.

8.5 Four Tips on how to Self-Regulate when you're Anxiously Attached

8.5.1 Manage Anger

A practical anger management approach can be to address one's anger in a way that is more beneficial to one's relationship with their spouse. This method of anger management is effective since it helps the relationship to become more stable and advanced. It is important to be straightforward with your spouse about the activities that anger you. This course of action is preferable to repressing your anger inside yourself or allowing it to fester until it can no longer be controlled and is released on your partner. A person with an anxious attachment style may find it advantageous to communicate with their partner by saying one of the following three things:

"Below is a list of causes for my irritation. It is possible that you will have difficulty understanding, but for some reason, it genuinely bothers me. I have no idea why."

"I feel like I have been harmed. I am aware that it is improbable that you meant for it to occur, but I am nonetheless concerned about the course of our relationship."

"To avoid a similar incident from occurring again, I was wondering if it were possible for us to communicate more often."

Be aware that some scripts, which may be advantageous for a securely attached partner, may trigger a partner who is avoidantly attached since these individuals fear growing too close to others. Due to their compatibility, a person with an anxious attachment type may realize that a person with a strong bond can be the perfect partner. They can comprehend the requirements of their partnership, and as a result, they can assist with regulating their partner's emotions. Because self-regulation demands a pause between a feeling and an action, a few techniques may help you focus more on what is happening inside your mind and body before attempting to regulate your emotions unpleasantly. Following are the relevant tactics:

8.5.2 Resolve to focus your attention consistently

This tactic requires us to pause, take a breath, and put some distance between what we are experiencing and our immediate response to these emotions. Mindfulness is the capacity to be aware and present of where we are and what we do at any given time. As a result, you will not become angry, needy, or clingy; instead, you will feel more relaxed and tranquil.

8.5.3 Reframe your current perspective on the situation

This strategy, also referred to as cognitive reframing, involves modifying your way of thinking to improve your self-regulation skills. This method aims to assist you in better managing your emotions and behaviors. This may be performed by mentally preparing yourself for the negative thoughts and emotions you are likely to experience, and then writing them down. The next stage is to examine facts that directly contradict these assumptions in order to refute them. For example, a person with an anxious attachment style may believe, "If I let my partner know how I feel, they will leave me." Consider a period when you were open and honest with your spouse about your emotions; what happened as a result? Once you get this understanding, you can replace the thinking contributing to your negative mood with more cheerful thoughts. This will help you control your unpleasant emotions and thoughts by grounding them in your relationship's reality. This will be pretty helpful to you in this endeavor.

8.5.4 Give therapy a chance

Through therapy, you may be able to comprehend the circumstances that led to your poor self-regulation strategies. Together with the support of a therapist, you may identify the triggers of your attachments and develop non-destructive methods for coping with your feelings that will not harm you or your relationship. To advance your recovery, you have access to in-person and online attachment repair support groups and courses.

8.6 Becoming More Attuned

The next step in overcoming anxious attachment triggers is to confront your past and process any unpleasant experiences or memories you have shut out. This may be accomplished by addressing your prior experiences and working through them. Keeping in mind that the ultimate goal of managing anxious attachment triggers is to prevent getting triggered and to work towards attunement as a method of coping, the first stage in managing anxious attachment triggers is to address your past. Because those of us who have experienced significant trauma may have lost the ability to feel anything to an intense degree, you must work on this. You will never be able to attune yourself to others or have meaningful interactions with them if you lack the emotional sensitivity to experience what others are feeling.

Therefore, to re-establish this sensitivity, you must first endure and recover from the unpleasant experience. You may start the healing process in one of two ways: either by processing the loss alone during an isolated time of grieving or by doing so in the presence of a significant other. The ultimate objective is to be able to reflect on the experience with calmness and happiness. Once you have had the opportunity to grieve and process old experiences and emotions, you will be ready to take the essential action steps toward minimizing triggers. Consequently, you will be able to take the appropriate action steps towards healing.

8.6.1 How to Heal Anxious Attachment Triggers

1. Utilize positive affirmations

Affirmations are declarations or comments that give you the psychological support and motivation you need. I want to share with you some particular affirmations that I have found beneficial for anxious attachment. It would be best if you began using them as soon as you feel awkward or uncomfortable. This will aid in retraining your neurological system.

Several affirmations that may be useful in addressing anxious attachment are as follows:

- You have earned the privilege. Since the moment of your birth, you have been deserving, and that status will never change.

- Right now, you have inside you all you need to feel quiet, calm, and in sync with the current circumstance.

- Do not fret about it. I admire you.

- Take several calm, deep breaths. Each time you take a deep breath, you get closer to having unshakable self-confidence, a solid sense of self, and healthy self-esteem.

- You can create a strong connection with others and become attuned to them.

1. Focus on learning about and tuning in to the other person in order to communicate successfully.

After experiencing a great deal of loss and working through the trauma, I have discovered that leading with my knowledge has been the most helpful factor in healing my neurological attachment patterns. This implies that in your talks and connections in general, you replace your sensations of anxiety (your triggers) with a sense of your partner's, spouse's, or family member's environment. You do this by empathizing with them and seeing yourself in their position. This can be a very effective form of anxiety relief. Because being anxiously connected implies that you have a propensity to focus on your issues (which, it must be acknowledged, can send you around in circles), it is very beneficial to focus on something you can control rather than letting your mind stray to your worries. You have total control over your ability to connect your ideas and values with those of the people you care about, as well as your intention and success. You must be aware that the great majority of the time, anxiously attached individuals create a variety of horrifying scenarios inside their own minds (that are more related to past abandonment than the present). This waste of energy might have been used to establish a meaningful relationship with another individual.

As soon as you become aware that worrying sensations are forming inside you, transfer your attention to the other person. Dedicate considerable time to listening to them and gauging their current state. The following questions may assist you in becoming better attuned to the other person and, as a result, feeling emotionally at ease:

- Where do they now stand regarding their priorities?

- Do they have a place for you in their lives, or do they even consider the possibility that they could?

You must be truthful with yourself and ask yourself the following questions in order to determine if the investment of your time and emotions is worthwhile:

- Do they care about how their actions may affect you?

- Has it ever been shown that they care (beyond doing what is convenient for themselves)?

8.7 How to Work through Anxious Attachment: Know the Goal

Your ultimate goal should be to steadily develop your ability to become attuned to others while simultaneously building stronger relationships. In order to have genuine feelings of attraction and an emotional connection in future love relationships, you must first become attuned to yourself. Maintaining any other fundamental connection in your life for an extended period is also necessary, making it an essential factor to consider. It can be challenging to have these two fundamental elements in a romantic relationship (emotional attraction and emotional connection). Hence it is illogical to expect a romantic relationship to remain stable and passionate for an extended period. These two fundamental elements of a love connection cannot exist without attunement. This is because your worries will interfere with your relationships, causing you to sabotage them out of stress, tension, or a general fear of abandonment. Again, this is since your anxieties will get in the way.

Aside from minimizing your anxiety, the principal objective here is to develop into a healthy and emotionally attuned human being. If you can achieve attunement, you will be not only able to develop connections with yourself but also with other individuals. Because you are an anxiously connected individual, the second item of utmost importance is for you to recognize that your attunement skills are fundamentally inadequate. This is something you must be aware of in all circumstances.

8.8 Warning: Attaching Early while Dating is Different to Having Anxious Attachment

Due to their feminine nature, women tend to form attachments early in relationships; this is especially prominent in younger women. It is possible to connect early and feel confident in your attachment, but it is also possible to connect early if you are the kind of person who battles with attachment anxiety. These are two distinct issues that need two distinct approaches. If you are a woman who suffers from anxious attachment, dating will likely be much more challenging than it already is.

8.9 Four Tips to Help Adults with Avoidant Attachment Self-Regulate in a Healthy Way

8.9.1 Take personal space when you need it

In a relationship, particularly one on the verge of getting more serious, giving each other emotional space is important. It may even help the relationship progress. This is particularly true when a disagreement is on the verge of escalating.

If you get the sense that an argument is imminent, you may want to say the following things to your partner:

"Listen, things are starting to heat up around here right now. I was wondering if it would be possible for us to take a little break and then address the matter."

"I want to begin by expressing my appreciation for the fact that you are always there for me, and then I would like to assure you that we will discuss this matter as soon as I am prepared to do so."

"I am fully aware that our discussion on this topic is of the highest importance; yet, I feel I must take a minute to gather my thoughts before we begin."

"In our romantic relationship, many things work in our favor. So, first, let us take a moment to assess our surroundings, and then we will continue discussing them from where we left off."

Keep in mind however, that since anxious people prefer to feel close to others, expressing a wish for space may trigger a sense of threat.

8.9.2 Open your communication

A person with avoidant attachment is afraid of displaying intense emotions or seeming out of control. In order to properly co-regulate emotions, it is essential to be able to communicate relationship concerns openly and honestly. Good communication must be fostered for both sides in a relationship to feel comfortable voicing their issues without fear of being judged. Over time, adults with an avoidant attachment style will realize that it is better to share their emotions openly as opposed to bottling them up.

8.9.3 Combat with the inner critic

The way an avoidant attacher thinks, often known as their "inner critic," exacerbates their distrust of others and their concern that others who care about them will reject or blame them for expressing their emotions. This is because they afraid of being rejected or criticized for expressing emotions. A person with an avoidant or dismissive attachment style may develop self-regulation by critically examining the process of expressing emotions. Alternatively, they worry about how others will react if they express the feelings they are now experiencing out of fear of how others perceive them. On the other hand, they may have outstanding beliefs about themselves, which may be a front for self-deprecating emotions.

Given that one's awareness of these concepts may be limited at first, it may be beneficial to begin by developing the ability to recognize them, and then to challenge the belief.

To demonstrate this idea, let us say you thought, "I cannot allow myself to get too close to someone. They will just end up letting me down." Give it some thought and try to recall a moment when someone you cared about was there for you. As a result, you might come to the awareness that your inner critic is not always correct.

8.9.4 Try professional counseling

Through therapy, you may be able to comprehend the circumstances that led to your poor self-regulation strategies and your unhealthy self-regulation strategies. Together with the support of a therapist, you may identify the triggers of your attachments and develop non-destructive methods for coping with your feelings that will not harm you or your relationship.

8.10 Understanding Your Style of Relating When Triggered

When your emotions are high, it may seem that you have no option but to react in a certain way; it may appear that you have lost control. Even though you may be aware of your emotional reaction, you are powerless to stop it due to the interaction between the neurological system, the brain, and the memory centers.

8.10.1 Your carefully maintained attitude to people

Regarding emotional language in the context of relationships, the bonds you develop as a youngster are the most influential factor. People with a dismissive attitude often have a withdrawing personality trait, which indicates that they do not trust anybody to be there for them; they do it alone, and they see it as not that big of a deal anyhow. This individual has difficulty forming and maintaining relationships with others in the short and long term. Because they have a constant sense of uneasiness and unpredictability, people with a style that may be classified as anxious are always seeking new partnerships. They are desperate to speak with someone and get confirmation that everything is proceeding well. They believe they are helpless and unable to do anything on their own; in the absence of another person, they are nothing. They are forever in search of someone else's favor.

8.10.2 Your brain's stimuli response

Your "M.O.," which is an acronym for the constant fallback mechanism that you use whenever there is tension or discord in a relationship, may comprise behaviors that occur in rapid succession. You am likely not "responding" as opposed to "reacting" because the primary distinction between the two terms relates to two distinct regions of the brain. You are not "responding" to the circumstance; rather, you are "reacting" to it. The emotional core, also known as the limbic system, is responsible for the emotions, while the logical core is responsible for your replies (cortex). When something elicits a reaction from you, the area of the brain responsible for higher-level cognition ceases to function; you might say it goes offline. To achieve this objective, the limbic and affective systems and the executive and cerebral systems must improve their communication.

Regardless of the substance of the "he said, she said" conversation, the first stage of this method is to become aware of the feelings that are occurring inside the body. The concentrated attention that is diverted to your internal somatic sensations, such as, "I notice my racing heart, the tension in my stomach, and I can feel my quick breath...," enables the essential pause to bring out the option of altering the pattern of constantly doing such and such. "I am aware of my beating heart…" "I can feel my tummy contracting…" "I am aware of my quick breathing." You may do this by focusing on the somatic sensations that develop inside your body. It is possible to learn how to intervene at any level of the interaction loop between the body's sensations, the nervous system, brain, emotions, ideas and beliefs, and your current behavior. This will allow you to develop new memories and generate new reactions.

If you have not processed and integrated your memories, the past does not belong to the past. Both forms of memory are stored in the same region of my brain: explicit and implicit. When people are aware of the specifics and realism of a former event, they are said to have explicit memory of that event. In addition to being prepared to react, components of implicit memory include the activation of my senses, emotions, perceptions, physical actions, and mental models at the moment of the event (generalized frame of reference for experience) (nervous system ready to respond to similar experience). Although the brain is packed with implicit memory, you are completely unaware of its existence. Integrating an implicit memory into the conscious and factual past of explicit memory requires the limbic and emotional brain region known as the hippocampus.

Changing emotional reactions, or "language," can lead to the triggers linked with your implicit memories; thus, you must learn how to respond differently when provoked. You must first intervene on a somatic or bodily level, which can re-inform the emotion; this has the power to re-inform the mental perspective, which has the potential to change the want to act on the drive toward old behavioral patterns. Whenever you are triggered and reminded of unresolved past difficulties, the body sends signals about a prior occurrence as if it were occurring right now. These communications are as though the event were occurring at this same now.

Consider the scenario in which our partner does not respond to us; for me, this evokes memories of how my father did not pay attention to us and ignored us; I experience the same sinking feeling in my stomach; the same feelings of anxiety, frustration, and hurt arise within me; and the negative self-perception of worthlessness triggers the cycle of negative self-talk in my head. I will likely act or react in a certain manner, grow upset and start shouting. My mental model and my priming would likely include using past knowledge to prepare me to take action to protect myself. If, on the other hand, I can exercise self-control over my emotions and re-inform myself with a new mental model and sensory experience, the new relational interaction that occurs internally and externally will result in the formation of a new memory.

After reconciling the fact that my mind, body, and heart are all working together to keep me safe, I will be able to investigate the information stored in my memory banks, determine how relevant it is, and begin the difficult process of regaining a more compassionate and conscious relationship with my reactivity. After acknowledging the rationale for my unreasonable behavior, I can achieve my objective. If I can learn how to grow my awareness above fundamental memory and survival level, my chances of connecting with my natural sense of safety, belonging, and connectivity will increase. If I can learn how to expand my awareness, I will be able to achieve this goal.

Chapter 9

MANAGING YOUR EMOTIONS

Every individual is constantly engaged in some connection and communication with the world around them, regardless of the circumstances. A great deal of activity may be occurring behind the scenes, influencing the quality of this contact and dialogue. These qualities may stem from the individual's attributes or another component of their environment. The quality of a person's connections with others may be impacted by various variables, such as prior experiences, personal traits, interests, attitudes, and expectations. In addition to everything else about the dynamics of interpersonal relationships, emotional intelligence is a subject that must be addressed. Over the last few years, the concept of emotional intelligence has been more prevalent across a vast array of professions. The American Dialect Society considered it one of the most advantageous newly created terms or phrases to emerge in the late 1990s.

9.1 Attachment Theory: Childhood, Adolescence, and Young Adulthood

According to attachment theory, a child's expectations and ideas about themselves, others, and their environment are impacted by the internal working models constructed in response to the quality of frequent attachment-related interactions with the parent. These encounters may occur in several settings, including play, discussion, and physical touch. Ainsworth's critical study defined three distinct forms of attachment in infants by observing how a youngster behaves when removed from and reunited with their primary caregiver. These three attachment types are secure, avoidant, and ambivalent. Children are more likely to build a secure attachment model if they encounter a sensitive caregiver who regularly meets their attachment requirements. This paradigm comprises self-representations of competence and judgments of others' dependability and accessibility in times of need. These encounters increase the likelihood that a child will build a stable attachment model. Conversely, children are less likely to develop a secure attachment model if they have not routinely interacted with a caregiver who meets their attachment needs.

A child is said to have an insecure-avoidance attachment connection with a primary caregiver when they have learned that showing distress or a desire for closeness during a challenging situation will likely result in rejection from the primary caregiver. This holds for youngsters who have acquired this knowledge via experience. Avoidant children often suppress attachment-related behaviors in order to shield themselves from the danger of rejection. These behaviors include the repressing of unpleasant feelings and the need for physical closeness. Children inclined to shun social interaction are more prone to develop a positive but erroneous self-perception due to their experiences, placing an undue emphasis on their capacity to handle challenging circumstances on their own.

As a consequence, they may learn to see other people as unreliable. Insecure and ambivalent children, on the other hand, have received inconsistent or unexpected care, which has led them to be apprehensive about whether or not their attachment figure will respond to their pain. Furthermore, due to their experiences as caretakers, ambivalent children can exaggerate and amplify their distress signals to maintain a strong relationship with their parents. As a result, these youngsters may perceive themselves as weak and unlovable, and may distrust others.

Later, Main and Solomon identified a fourth attachment form, which they termed insecure-disorganized. According to one school of thinking, children may develop an attachment problem if their parents exhibit fearful or terrifying behavior. According to Main and Hesse, insecure children are in a precarious position where the thing that provides them with the most incredible comfort also causes them the most distress. When these young toddlers are distressed, they display not simply unclear but also conflicting behaviors toward their attachment figure.

In addition, children with disorganized attachments have the most significant degree of emotion dysregulation, and lack organized and coherent attachment strategies for seeking parental contact during stressful situations. Because of these traits, disorganized attachments are the least desired form. Due to these characteristics, they are regarded as the weakest attachment type.

Some categorization approaches for adolescent attachment models include categorical and continuous security aspects, while others emphasize continuous security scales. Other categorization methods exist for various kinds of adolescent attachment. As a result, a more self-confident adolescent is more likely to participate in a goal-corrected relationship with a parent. This interaction allows the adolescent to attain regular age-appropriate social objectives such as developing peer relationships, broader exploration of a more extensive environment, etc., while at the same time, maintaining open communication with his or her parents. However, increased attachment insecurity among adolescents toward their parents is characterized by bitterness and estrangement in addition to emotional distance.

Throughout this crucial development period, the adolescent's parents remain the primary attachment figure; yet, the adolescent's close friends increasingly provide specific attachment demands. Following this notion, those who investigated participants' (aged 6 to 17) preferred attachment figures concerning the four components of attachment (i.e., proximity seeking, haven, separation distress, and secure base) found that nearly all participants preferred spending time with their peers over their parents. In addition, individuals between the ages of 8 and 14 demonstrated an increasing preference for receiving comfort and emotional support from their peers. This trend remained even when the subjects reached 14 years of age. However, the participants' parents remained the leading sources of security and causes of separation-related suffering. The researchers discovered that romantic partners were unanimously acknowledged as the preferred attachment figures throughout the later stages of adolescence.

Attachment in romantic relationships between adults may be analyzed along two orthogonal dimensions that examine general sentiments and perceptions regarding romantic partners. These factors may be used to gauge attachment in romantic relationships between adults. These characteristics include intolerance to physical closeness and abandonment anxiety. People with an avoidant attachment style often deeply mistrust their love relationships and find physical proximity to others upsetting. On the other hand, those with an anxious attachment style are apprehensive about the probability that their partners may leave them. As a result, these individuals exhibit little confidence in their relationships. When seen together, a person's parents, peers, and romantic partners all play significant roles as attachment figures throughout various stages of development. The term major attachment figures is especially appropriate in this situation.

9.2 Attachment Styles as a Predictor of Emotional Intelligence

In recent years, research on emotional intelligence has blossomed in both the fundamental and applied psychology domains, with methods in the latter field presenting emotional intelligence as a solution for contemporary business and education issues. Emotional intelligence is the capacity to identify and express one's emotions, as well as to regulate and manage them, and make efficient use of emotional information in one's thinking and behavior. This kind of intelligence plays a big role in the degree of happiness that individuals report experiencing in their daily encounters. Alternately, emotional intelligence may be defined as the capacity to control one's emotions while simultaneously using the power inherent within them. Individuals seek to change their circumstances via behavioral control, aided by emotional considerations. It is not sufficient to have sensations; one must also be able to explain and transmit them.

Emotional intelligence, often known as EQ, is a factor that contributes to our observation and evaluation of our own and others' emotions, as well as the reflection of the information and energy that emotions provide to our daily lives and activities.

People may be deemed emotionally intelligent if they can use their emotions effectively to achieve their objectives, whether linked to their job, education, or day-to-day life. Goleman, who is credited with developing the term, identified five key components of emotional intelligence. The first three aspects pertain to an individual's capacity to govern himself, while the last two pertain to their ability to manage their interactions with others. Later, he and his colleagues whittled down the five dimensions of emotional intelligence, which originally included twenty-five competencies, to four dimensions, including nineteen abilities. This reduction decreased the number of emotional intelligence abilities to four.

Boyatzis and colleagues grouped these characteristics into their categories, naming them self-awareness, self-management, social awareness, empathy, and social skills. Self-awareness may be broken down into its constituent pieces, which include knowing one's own emotions, wants, resources, and intuitions. This dimension encompasses the competencies of emotional self-awareness, correct self-evaluation, and self-confidence. Self-management is the process of exerting control over one's ideas, emotions, and impulses, as well as one's resources, to attain one's objectives more effectively. Social awareness is the ability to comprehend and empathize with the experiences, emotions, and concerns of others. According to Goleman and

Dolmen, empathy is the most useful attribute regarding one's capacity to connect to others.

One of the most crucial components of having strong social skills is the ability to elicit the desired response from others. This category includes the skills of leadership, communication, influence, functioning as a catalyst for change, conflict management, relationship building, cooperation and collaboration, and developing others. There is a correlation between a person's degree of emotional intelligence and several other elements of their lives, such as the quality of their interpersonal relationships, their level of success in their careers, and their general happiness. As a result of his research in the next years, Bar-On suggests an emotional-social intelligence method. Bar-On suggests analyzing it as an emotional-social intelligence rather than separate concepts of emotional and social intelligence. According to Bar-On, emotional and social intelligence are intrinsically linked.

Emotional-social intelligence, or ESI, is a collection of interrelated emotional and social competencies, skills, and facilitators that determines how well we understand and express ourselves, how well we understand others and communicate with them, and how well we can manage the demands of daily life. ESI is a cross-section of emotionally and socially linked competencies, skills, and facilitators. The phrases emotional and social skills, abilities, and facilitators are used interchangeably in this approach. Below is a list of the five components that comprise the referred-to emotional and social skills, talents, and facilitators: intrapersonal intelligence, adaptation, stress management, and general mood emotional intelligence sub-dimensions. Self-respect, emotional self-awareness, assertiveness, independence, and self-actualization are indicators of an individual's intrapersonal emotional intelligence.

Individuals with a high degree of intrapersonal emotional intelligence are in touch with their emotions, readily able to articulate their thoughts and emotions, and control their behavior. Individuals with strong intrapersonal emotional intelligence also possess high interpersonal emotional intelligence. Components of an individual's interpersonal emotional intelligence include empathy, social responsibility, and the ability to maintain strong interpersonal ties. High levels of interpersonal emotional intelligence enable individuals to comprehend the emotional expressions of others, communicate successfully, and get along well with others. They are also capable of understanding how their own emotions manifest. Adaptability is a component of emotional intelligence comprising three subcomponents: the capacity to solve problems, the ability to test reality, and flexibility. Control of one's impulses and stress resistance the skill to deal with stressful conditions is a component of emotional intelligence. The typical demeanor of these individuals might be defined as ice-cold. Temperament, contentment, and a positive outlook are fundamental components of emotional intelligence.

According to Bar-On, this model is comprised of the following characteristics: the ability to be emotionally and socially intelligent; knowing oneself and being able to express oneself effectively; knowing others and forming positive relationships with them; and successfully coping with the demands, challenges, and pressures of daily life. In actuality, an individual's day-to-day social behavior is strongly correlated with his or her level of emotional self-control. Numerous factors may influence a person's degree of self-awareness, as well as their ability to express themselves, their ability to connect with others, and their disposition toward optimism. Because humans are social beings, our family, friends, and educational experiences may all significantly impact the development of these talents. Early experiences significantly impact the emotional intelligence skills that individuals acquire throughout their lives.

According to Bar-On, Trek, and Yeşilyaprak, emotional intelligence is a trait that can be developed and should not be neglected. Furthermore, it is something that has an opportunity for improvement. During the first years of a person's existence, their interactions with their surroundings have the greatest potential to define their identity. During this stage, a person's identity is most likely to develop. Bowlby was the first person to propose a model of the mother-child interaction, and this model integrates Bowlby's functions. The Bowlby model was first suggested in 1973 and then again in 1982. Primarily, it is believed that the child and mother have evolved a synchronized connection in which the mother recognizes the infant's distress or fear signals and provides comfort, protection, and a stable foundation from which the infant may explore the surroundings. This synchronized connection between the mother and baby is thought to begin during the infant's first few weeks.

According to Bowlby, early experiences of care are internalized as functional models. These models not only serve as a template for future interactions with others but also provide unspoken standards for how an individual should experience, express, and cope with uncomfortable emotions. Bowlby defines attachment as a child's strong inclination to seek intimacy and contact with a specific figure under certain situations, especially when he is fearful, weary, or ill. Attachment may be seen in a child's behavior during worried, fatigued, or ill states. Bowlby argued that the behavior of attachment has its specific dynamics, separate from both the behavior of feeding and the behavior of sexuality, and has at least equal importance in a human's existence. Attachment behavior is ultimately responsible for developing emotional bonds between a child and his or her parents.

9.3 The Security of Attachment in Terms of Emotions

Secure attachment is connected with several good psychological outcomes in early childhood, including more positive peer relationships, a positive sense of self, a better knowledge of emotions, and an increased ability to address social difficulties. In order to treat many of these psychological consequences, the patient must learn the capacity to self-regulate their emotions. Multiple studies have found that a secure parent-child attachment is related to inhibited toddlers' lower cortisol reactivity in challenging situations, better anger management strategies in preschoolers, and greater constructive coping with stress in middle childhood. These results are consistent with the theoretical position that parental sensitivity and responsiveness contribute to stable attachment and improved emotion self-regulation in children by assisting them when they struggle to regulate their negative emotions.

In other words, the data support the concept that parental sensitivity leads to a child's safe attachment and more robust emotional self-regulation. In addition to the parent's direct attention to their child's needs, however, there are additional ways in which parents with secure attachment behaviors might help children develop greater emotion control. These techniques are comparable to how safe attachment develops in adulthood. Parents with strong attachments to their children are likely to have a more accurate and observant grasp of their children's emotions and the variables that contribute to them, allowing them to give more beneficial assistance to their children. This is because parents with strong ties to their children generally also have strong relationships. They may have conversations with the youngster, during which they may share profound knowledge of helpful coping mechanisms. This talk might occur about the time they both had. In summary, research indicates that the traits associated with a secure attachment contribute to developing healthy emotion regulation in infants.

9.4 Attachment and Maternal Emotion Attributions

Depending on the context, parental involvement in regulating their children's emotions, which includes training self-control methods, may be both preventative and reactive. In contrast, the effectiveness of the adult's judgment of the child's actual or anticipated emotions is essential for successfully implementing these interventions The child's emotional reaction to the parent's activities will vary.

The fact that relatively little research has been conducted to investigate the accuracy of parental perceptions of young children's emotional experiences may be explained by the assumption that correctly decoding a child's emotional experience should be a simple prerequisite for supporting emotion regulation. The results of a 1999 study conducted by Levine and colleagues shed light on why the perspectives of adults and young people are not always the same. Parents and their preschool-aged children were given independent cues to recollect recent situations they had discussed, during which the child felt happiness, sadness, anger, or fear. Separate cues were sent to parents and preschool-aged children. The rate of agreement between the predominant emotion stated by a parent and the child differed depending on whether the parent had recorded pleasure (0.80), sadness (0.72), fear (0.49), or anger. The rate of concurrence varied from happiness (0.80) to sadness (0.72) to fear (0.49) to rage (0.49).

Subsequent studies found that one of the most frequent causes of conflicts between parents and children was that the adults presented contradicting accounts of the child's intentions during the occurrence, resulting in differing emotional interpretations from each side. This was one of the leading causes of conflict between parents and children. It was more probable that the mother would disagree with the child if her emotional assessment of the child was based on differing assumptions of the child's aspirations in that particular context. There are further instances in which a parent's emotional state may give rise to opinions that conflict with the feelings their child is experiencing. Several studies have shown, for instance, that depressive women react to their children's emotions in ways that are consistent with criticism and a feeling of helplessness. It is likely that, as a consequence, the mothers will have an erroneous understanding of what their children are experiencing.

We investigated the concordance of child and maternal perceptions of the child's feelings during an emotion regulation probe, as well as the origins of individual differences in mother-child agreement because accurate decoding of a young child's emotions is crucial for parental efforts to support emotion regulatory efforts of offspring. Specifically, we were interested in whether child and mother views of a child's emotions during an emotion control investigation were congruent. The emotion control probe consisted of a method in which the child got a sweet or snack of his or her choosing, which the youngster was permitted to consume with the mother's consent; however, mothers were told individually to postpone the child's consumption until much later. The youngster was then permitted to eat with the mother's approval. The subsequent exchanges between mothers and children centered on the mother denying the child's request and assisting the child in coping with the unpleasant emotions caused by the mother's choice. After some time had passed, the mother and child were asked how they felt throughout the procedure and why they felt the way they did. The mother and child were each given a video recording of their actions throughout the process. We expected that there would be some discrepancies between maternal and child accounts of the child's feelings during the denied request task, even though each participant was seeing a videotape of a scenario that had happened recently and in which the child's purpose was evident and unambiguous.

We hypothesized that there would be individual differences in the degree to which mothers and children agreed on some issues and that four other factors would influence these individual differences. The first component was the consistency of the mother-child connection, which was based on a significant body of research indicating that moms of securely attached children are more sensitive to their children's emotions and needs. The second factor was maternal depressive symptomatology, based on earlier research indicating that sad moms had distorted perceptions of their children's emotional states. The association between the two parameters was attributed to this investigation. As a potential predictor of children's perceptions of emotion, the mothers' representations of emotion in their own lives were investigated to see whether they might throw light on the subject. In particular, their views on the importance of recognizing and appreciating one's emotional experiences were considered. They emphasized the significance of this point.

The meta-emotion philosophy that parents contribute to their children's emotion management is based on their views on the relevance of emotion in their lives. This contributed to the explanation for why this was the case. This foundation was one of the pillars upon which this edifice was erected. It is more probable that parents will pay attention to how their children feel if they recognize the importance of emotions in their lives and think their feelings deserve to be respected. This concept, which relates to how mothers perceive the feelings their children are experiencing, has never been the subject of an empirical examination until now. Fourth, we considered the impact the child may have had on the mother and child's capacity to agree on the child's emotional experience. Based on our results, we hypothesized that children with a greater understanding of their own negative emotions are more likely to convey and define these sensations more accurately, hence contributing to a higher degree of mother-child concordance.

9.5 Attachment and Child Conversational Avoidance

When parents have dialogues with their children about emotionally stimulating situations from the past, they contribute to developing their children's capacity to exert control over their emotions. In the socialization of emotion regulation, having retrospective memories of events that occurred in the recent past has several benefits over direct parental interventions. These events must have occurred during the last few years. When young children have some emotional distance from the heightened arousal they are experiencing, it is more likely that they will listen to and follow their parents' advice. In addition, the back-and-forth exchange of ideas between a parent and a child during conversation provides more excellent opportunities for enhancing children's developing knowledge about emotion regulation in the context of a broader understanding of emotion, social rules regarding emotional displays, and the effects of these displays on others.

Significant research documents the importance of the topic and quality of conversation between parents and preschoolers on preschoolers' development of an understanding of emotion, and in a similar vein, the topic and quality of conversation between parents and preschoolers influences preschoolers' development of an understanding of how to control their emotions. Parents tend to discuss negative emotions with their young children more often than positive ones. This may be because young children find negative sensations more perplexing than happy ones, as well as the fact that negative sentiments are typically the focus of parental attempts to control young children's behavior.

Long ago, specialists who investigated interactions between parents and children on traumatic events in the child's life recognized that young children often opt not to discuss recent bad experiences. To escape the matter, they abruptly change the subject, evade their mother's worries, quit the situation, or flat-out refuse to engage in further discourse. Remembering that this is a typical response to a mother's encouragement to discuss difficult or distressing topics is vital. Therefore, parents must adapt their conversational style to overcome their children's predisposition to avoid talking about emotionally distressing events. This is because such conversations provide the chance to discuss strategies for emotion control.

In order to further our knowledge of how parent-child talks impact the development of emotional awareness and emotion regulation in children, it is crucial to explore the variables that induce young children to avoid discussing unpleasant feelings with their moms. We were particularly interested in three criteria that influence the incidence of evasion. The first hypothesis examined the stability of a connection and hypothesized that infants with stable attachments to their mothers demonstrate less avoidance behavior than children who lacked such links. This conclusion is consistent with the theory that mothers and children with stable connections have more open, fluid communication that permits more emotional sharing and conversation, especially of negative feelings that may be more upsetting, unsettling, or perplexing for young children. This finding indicates that mothers and children with secure relationships engage in more open, fluid communication that facilitates greater emotional sharing and discussion.

The second element was the mother's support of the child's perspective throughout their chat. This hypothesis was founded on the assumption that more validating moms would give young children a more comfortable and welcoming interpersonal context in which to share grief or rage experienced in the past. Third, this hypothesis was founded on the assumption that more affirming moms would encourage young children to discuss their emotions. This hypothesis is based on the notion that there is a link between more validating mothers and the availability of opportunities for young children to share their feelings. Due to its greater relevance to the issue, we focused our efforts on the children's perception of negative emotions. Our study revealed that youngsters who understand negative feelings are more inclined to discuss their emotional experiences. This indicates that children's emotional cognition is likely to affect their readiness to discuss emotional experiences substantially. Moreover, we investigated the relationship between child avoidance and depressive symptoms, as well as the mother's emotional representations.

9.6 Attachment and Psychopathology

Individuals' internal working models of early attachment relationships influence their perceptions of themselves and others and their resistance and susceptibility to stressful life events, influencing their well-being and mental health. It has been shown that persons with insecure attachment models have more entrenched ideas of themselves and more negative and skewed attitudes and expectations of others. As a result of these erroneous cognitive models, people may perceive and feel complicated and stressful events in a more negative manner (such as anger, anguish, disappointment, despair, jealousy, and helplessness), which may exacerbate their suffering. These individuals may also be more susceptible to negative emotional responses, including anger, pain, disappointment, despair, and a sense of helplessness. Attachment security throughout childhood, adolescence, and early adulthood is a protective factor against psychopathology and associated symptoms, including anxiety, sadness, dissociation, and antisocial behaviors. Participants were tracked from infancy through early adulthood for this study. This hypothesis is congruent with the finding that connection security during various stages of development is a protective factor against particular outcomes.

On the other hand, it is believed that internalized images of oneself and others that developed due to insensitive caring enhance the likelihood of developmental maladaptation throughout one's life. Attachment insecurity is thus seen as a significant risk factor for adult psychopathology, which may emerge as symptoms of anxiety, depression, dissociation, and antisocial behavior. Attachment insecurity, on the other hand, is not considered a disorder in and of itself but rather a significant risk factor for adult psychopathology.

Because different attachment figures, such as parents and peers, play an active role in the adolescent's life during this stage of development, it is an exciting developmental stage to study in terms of attachment insecurity and psychopathology, as mentioned previously. Adolescence is one of the most intriguing phases of development. In ongoing and planned studies with teenage samples, attachment insecurity has been related to increased rates of depression and behavioral issues. For instance,

Lee and Hankin found that anxious and avoidant attachment orientations to parents and close friends in adolescence predicted future increases in depressed and anxious symptoms over five months. This was true for adolescents who exhibited anxious and avoidant attachment orientations toward both their parents and close friends.

This research lacked an analysis of the independent effect of attachment security on parents and peers; instead, it relied on a global attachment score to define the degree of attachment. In two further studies incorporating independent parent and peer evaluations, both attachment links were shown to be concurrently associated with psychopathology. The United Kingdom and the United States performed these studies. Higher levels of general insecurity were associated with increased anxiety and depression in adolescents, while higher levels of security were associated with better levels of overall adjustment. Attachment to one's parents and attachment to one's peers had the same effect in connection to psychopathology, according to the findings of both of these studies. Finally, Wilkinson and Walford performed research where they observed that adolescent attachment security was only associated with reduced distress when maintained with parents and not peers. When all of the study results are taken together, it is evident that they do not entirely agree on the specific effect that insecure attachment to one's parents and peers has on the formation of psychopathology-related symptoms. Due to the cross-sectional nature of these investigations, our knowledge of the longitudinal impact of particular associations on later adult psychopathology is limited. This constrains our capacity to make any conclusions.

Research has also been undertaken to examine if an association exists between increased attachment insecurity in adulthood and overall psychopathology; however, the results of these investigations are contradictory. According to various research findings, the intensity of an individual's internalizing, externalizing, and overall symptoms are positively correlated with either an anxious or an avoidant attachment style. Others show higher connections between the anxious component and psychopathology symptoms than the avoidant dimension, especially when internalizing symptoms (such as anxiety and depression) are quantified as outcomes. This is especially true when comparing the anxious dimension to the avoidant dimension.

As noted in the preceding conclusion, attachment insecurity is associated with various psychopathological symptoms in adolescence and adulthood. However, to the best of our knowledge, there has been no investigation into the links between these two periods of development. In addition, the research conducted on teenagers regarding the relative effect of attachment to parents vs. attachment to peers, as well as the study conducted on adults regarding the relative influence of anxious versus avoidant orientations on outcome measures, is inconsistent. In the United States, research has been performed in both fields. In addition, most of the study has been on the relationship between attachment patterns and symptoms of mental health disorders like anxiety and depression. Contrary to popular belief, it is not preferable when studying nonclinical populations to analyze general symptoms of psychopathology rather than particular disorders.

Chapter 10

FORGIVING YOURSELF

As we have learned throughout this book, individuals with negative attachment experiences as children are more likely to lack the necessary skills to develop successful adult relationships. Poets and academics have been preoccupied with the theme of love for a considerable amount of time. The concept of "love" has been investigated on three psychological levels: platonic, friendly, and romantic. There are also four unique types of love:

- Attachment love, which refers to an infant's innate need to remain close to his or her caregiver for protection

- Compassionate love, which refers to an altruistic, innate desire to create bonds with others for emotional support during times of distress

- Companionate love/liking, which refers to the process by which friendships are formed based on a reward and punishment system, which is divided into categories of familiarity, similarity, and attractiveness

- Romantic love

Forgiveness can be essential in forming and preserving relationships. Patterns of forgiveness are taught simultaneously with the development of a baby's attachment type. This occurs as children approach adolescence and spend more time participating in social activities with others. The process of forgiving someone includes your emotions and choices. In order to forgive, it is vital to make a conscious effort to move from negative to positive feelings. Caregivers and other role models have the opportunity to train children on how to develop emotional healing abilities when relationship traumas occur.

Much research has been undertaken on the association between an individual's attachment style and the romantic and committed love relationships they have experienced as an adult. In addition to the study on attachment type and forgiveness, a substantial amount of research has also been conducted on the issue of forgiveness and consummate love relationships. These studies may be found in Allemand, Amberg, and other sources.

10.1 Love

Depending on the circumstances, distinct individuals may interpret the concept of love to signify a wide variety of different things. People may speak about how much they love their grandparents, pets, siblings, romantic partners, or favorite television series, but the emotional significance underpinning each of these bonds is unique. The study of love has led to the development of several theories that attempt to explain how and why we love other humans, animals, objects, and concepts. It has been suggested that love acts as a bridge between the ideal and real self, a system of positive reinforcement, an instinctual impulse that leads to sex, a path to the divine that provides pure benevolence, and an evolutionary bonding process that provides mutual protection and safety. There are so many different kinds of loving relationships, so it may not be easy to describe how and why individuals love one another.

Love is a process that people go through in order to feel connected to others in some manner. It is possible to state this with total confidence. Robert Sternberg believed that any healthy romantic relationship should have passion, intimacy, and dedication. A common definition of passion includes desire, attraction, heightened arousal, and a sense of romance. A component of the intimate experience is the feeling of connectivity, the establishment of links, and the perception that one's significant other is very well known.

Commitment needs various essential elements, such as the desire to love, the ability to continue loving, the readiness to make sacrifices, and the will to stop searching for other prospective partners. There are partnerships with just one or two of these elements, but a healthy and fruitful consummate relationship will have all three.

Love devoid of commitment in a romantic relationship is empty of value. Although both partners may have decided to be together for a longer time, this does not necessarily mean desire or closeness. This may be the case in a married couple that has been together for a long time but no longer has the emotional or romantic connection they once had. This may also be the case with arranged marriages, in which the partners are dedicated to one another but do not have an intimate or passionate relationship. In these contexts, it is hard to describe the marriage as passionate or intimate.

Infatuation is the overpowering feeling between a couple when their love connection is dominated by desire. Profound sentiments of yearning mark this kind of relationship. A biological attraction and a longing for one another are likely the driving forces behind this connection. When these characteristics are present in a relationship between two people, their connection is more comprehensive.

A romantic relationship that does not involve commitment from either party is characterized by physical intimacy and sexual desire between the parties. During a romantic relationship, two individuals may fall in love. However, this love may be brief, and the relationship itself may not last for a long time. A healthy companionate relationship requires an intimate bond and a dedication to the partnership. This term describes friendships that last for extended periods, sometimes even a lifetime, despite the absence of a physical attraction between the persons involved. The relationships between families members who have consented to remain in one other's lives are another kind of relationship that falls under this category.

Despite great feelings of love and devotion, a relationship is doomed to fail if there is a lack of intimacy between the two persons involved. This pattern occurs in romantic relationships between persons who have experienced love at first sight but do not know one another well enough to develop an intimate bond. This love may also be ephemeral, but it has a chance of lasting if the two persons involved can develop a deeper emotional connection over time. These characteristics must coexist for gratifying romantic relationship. In addition to being passionately and sexually attracted to one another, people in these relationships are dedicated to being with one another for an extended period, feel connected to one another, and have a friendship with one another.

Diessner, Frost, and Smith examined whether Sternberg's theory of love is consistent with neoclassical philosophical notions of the human mind. Specifically, the researchers investigated eros, a sensation that might be defined as love at first sight. According to their investigation's results, the two seem to have some shared characteristics. Plato's interpretations of Socrates' teachings deconstructed the human mind into three distinct parts: logiston, thymia, and epithymia. Sternberg's commitment theory is consistent with the cognitive and volitional process he calls logiston. Sternberg refers to this process as logiston. Thymia is the sentimental and emotional portion of the human psyche associated with profound personal relationships. It may be seen as the ability for human love and compassion. Sternberg compares epithymia, a human desire, to the idea of passion. He refers to this desire as the passionate impulse. Numerous philosophers have explored the three components of the human mind, often known as knowledge, emotion, and desire or deliberate action. Sternberg's present theory of love was influenced by many philosophers throughout history, as seen by examining the intellectual origins of how humans feel love.

10.2 Forgiveness

Worthington and Wade described forgiveness as the victim's personal decision, conscious or unconscious, to abandon unforgiveness and seek reconciliation with the perpetrator if it is safe, sensible, and practicable to do so. The victim's internal decision, whether unconscious or conscious, is to release resentment and seek reconciliation with the perpetrator if it is safe, wise, and possible. On the other hand, unforgiveness is defined as a 'cold' emotion, including wrath, bitterness, and maybe hatred, associated with the deliberate avoidance of or retribution against a transgressor. Forgiveness techniques include replacing negative ideas, feelings, and behaviors with good ones or changing one's motives. In addition to releasing a negative emotion and replacing it with a good one, forgiveness is also the intentional process of resolving a problem in order to move on.

Worthington refers to these two types of forgiveness as emotional forgiveness and decisional forgiveness. When going through the phases that lead to whether or not to forgive another person, one may consider both the good and bad elements of forgiveness. There is a high likelihood that forgiving will open the door to many good possibilities and experiences if you choose to do so. It is possible that if you forgive someone, it will make it easier to let go of animosity and hate. This experience may also lead to the development of skills that will prevent a similar transgression from occurring in the future if the transgressor can learn from his or her mistake, acknowledge the compassion of the transgressed, and make more significant efforts to avoid making the same mistake again. A large number of individuals would conclude that forgiving others is compatible with their moral or spiritual beliefs.

Forgiveness is a societal expectation that has become so normalized in contemporary culture that cliches such as "forgive and forget" have developed. It has been shown that primates and other animals comprehend the social expectations of forgiving an offense. This has had several positive effects, including reestablishing the cohesive animal tribe, reducing social anxiety, and preventing animals from developing a sense of isolation.

According to some data, the advantages of human social groupings are equivalent to those of other social systems. Several studies have shown a substantial association between the capacity to forgive another person and their physical and mental wellbeing. On the other side, there are challenges associated with forgiving another person.

One factor that may make it difficult to forgive is the perception that if one forgives, he or she forfeits the ability to seek vengeance or exact revenge for wrongdoing. Some people may also consider forgiving someone as equivalent to condoning the transgression, and may wonder whether it encourages the transgressor to continue such violations. It might also be seen as a sign of weakness, a symptom of poor self-esteem, or even permission to absolve the transgressor of responsibility for their committed violation. There is also a possibility that seeking revenge is more for the good of society as a whole than for the victim's pleasure. If the transgressor is punished with retribution, they may be dissuaded from repeating the offense, perhaps against a different prospective victim.

10.3 Forgiveness in Attachment Styles

According to some research results, individuals with an insecure attachment style may be less likely to build healthy and meaningful romantic relationships as adults. In adult relationships, people with anxious attachment styles tend to be dependent, needy, and vulnerable. Adults with avoidant attachment styles are more likely to experience feelings of rejection, abandonment, and distance in romantic relationships. They are also less likely to seek assistance from their partners during times of emotional stress. Concerning the issue of passion, individuals with anxious attachment styles are more likely to become easily jealous of their partners or suffocate them, whereas individuals with avoidant attachment styles are more likely to show too little interest, which can make their partners feel rejected or unwanted. In turn, this may impact the amount of intimacy that the insecurely connected person's relationship feels; a lack of trust may result from having an overbearing spouse or a partner who shows little or no sexual interest in him or her. People who are insecure about themselves and their partners may feel unable to speak safely with one another, which may have a detrimental effect on their close relationships.

Additionally, an insecure attachment style might make it challenging to commit to a spouse. Anxious persons are more prone to become too reliant and less likely to offer their partners personal space, while avoidant ones are less likely to reach a place in a relationship where they can commit. The above sequence of events may elicit various unpleasant feelings, including anger, anxiety, uncertainty, pain, bewilderment, resentment, and even hate. However, by talking truthfully, demonstrating empathy, and forgiving someone who has harmed you, you may be able to replace your negative emotions with positive ones. As a result, forgiveness has the potential to function as a variable that mediates the association between attachment styles and adult romantic relationships.

PART 4 - SOME PARTING WORDS

To recap, someone is said to have fearful-avoidant attachment when they have a want for a connection but at the same time attempt to avoid having one. In other words, they desire a connection but also seek to avoid having one. There is a link between a baby's insecure attachment style and the attachment style of their parents. If you can gain knowledge of the nature of your attachment type, it may be feasible for you to build a more practical plan for dealing with love relationships. The unique collection of chromosomes that each human has, in addition to the experiences that they have had during their life, influences how they interact with other individuals.

Adults with difficulty forming healthy attachments tend to emotionally cut themselves off from others after becoming close to them. Such people often have an unhealed wound due to having been abandoned in the past, and breakups may be challenging for them. People with difficulties with anxiety, avoidance, or attachment could believe they deserved to be dumped after a relationship. It is conceivable that one day they may feel gloomy, and the following day they will feel emotionally disconnected. Both of these states are feasible. These individuals are driven by two opposing forces within themselves: one craves and demands connection, while the other is deeply suspicious of it and afraid of it. Such individuals are motivated by these forces because they cannot reconcile their conflicting emotions. As a result, it may be challenging to gain attention while interacting with someone with this attachment type.

It is possible to convey to another individual that you care about them by showing compassion and empathy for them in their time of need. Be sure to have an open mind and be prepared to accompany them to attachment-based couple's therapy sessions. As a consequence of this, you will be in a better position to guide them toward the development of their connection skills in an effective way.

If you want a healthy relationship with a fearful or evasive person, the three most crucial traits to build are honesty, patience, and trust. These qualities will allow you to establish a long-lasting and positive connection with that individual. These characteristics also make it more likely that a romantic partnership will be highly successful in the long run. If you see a difference in how your spouse uses their body language, you should not immediately assume that they are attempting to keep anything from you, even if you also notice a change in how they use their voice. You will improve your talents to communicate with others in the real world if you participate in activities of this kind. You should set some fair limits for your behavior and pay attention to the things that are going through your thoughts even when you are not consciously aware of them.

Many people with the attachment style known as fearful avoidant may have a skewed perception of what constitutes appropriate boundaries in their romantic relationships. This is because fearful avoidance is characterized by a tendency to withdraw emotionally from close relationships. Consider seeking the assistance of a trained expert by enrolling in counseling; doing so may assist you in modifying your attachment style and maturing into a person who is more at ease in their interactions with other people. CBT and other therapeutic approaches assist patients in recognizing and treating destructive patterns of thought, emotion, and behavior. When a person has a fearful-avoidant attachment style, it might be challenging for them to make a long-term commitment to another person. They have a propensity to steer clear of being engaged in significant relationships while at the same time seeking ways to connect with others. This dichotomy may make it difficult for them to achieve their goals.

They fear being too attached to others and placing their faith in them. People with an attachment style characterized by fear and avoidance are more prone to seek out casual sexual encounters. If things get too harsh for them, they may become reluctant to confront serious concerns or share an excessive quantity of personal information. In addition, if things continue to become more challenging, they may become quite withdrawn and become suspicious of their spouse. A person with a scared avoidant attachment style may be more prone to break a healthy love connection on their own out of dread and a mistaken sensation that they are in danger. This is because they perceive themselves in danger more often than they are.

It is essential to put in the effort to cultivate the ability to self-regulate one's thoughts and emotions. Only a tiny fraction of individuals are aware that how we relate to other people affects the degree to which we can exert control over our emotions.

The emphasis that contemporary society places on achieving success in one's career and on the traditional model of the nuclear family has led to the creation of environments that are less than optimal for the growth and development of infants, toddlers, and young children. People with an anxious attachment style may have had a caregiver who was unreliable or inconsistent in satisfying their needs when they were young. This might have contributed to the development of their attachment style. It is not just the absence of emotionally available parents to their children that plays a significant role in the development of individuals with insecure attachment patterns; isolation from other people also plays a significant role in this development. Adults who suffer from anxious attachments tend to concentrate on the possible dangers to their relationships, which may make it difficult for them to focus on anything else. In order to create and sustain healthy relationships, a person whose attachment style is anxious has to gain the skills required to learn how to self-regulate.

CONCLUSION

Someone is said to have fearful-avoidant attachment when they require a connection but at the same time attempt to avoid having one with another person. People who struggle with anxiety as adults often have the erroneous idea that other people do not find them likable and do not place value on them. Adults who struggle to create healthy relationships tend to emotionally withdraw from the people around them, making it more difficult for them to form good connections. When you love someone with a fearful attachment type, you naturally want to do all in your power to assist them in recognizing and coming to terms with the underlying challenges they face in life.

This requires pushing individuals to seek support to accomplish this task. Honesty, patience, and trust are three traits that must be cultivated to have a good relationship with a fearful or evasive person. Set some fair limits for your behavior and pay attention to the things going through your thoughts. It is also necessary that you create some appropriate boundaries for your conduct.

Consider signing up for counseling so that you may get assistance from someone trained to provide it.

A person with an attachment style known as fearful avoidant may be more inclined to leave a good romantic connection out of fear and an erroneous feeling that they are in danger. Adults who deal with anxious attachments tend to concentrate on the potential dangers to their relationships. This may be a very unhealthy way to think about these issues. A person who has an anxious attachment style has to learn how to self-regulate in order to be able to create and sustain healthy relationships. This is because anxious people find it difficult to manage their own emotions.

An insecure attachment can have repercussions throughout a child's life in the form of low self-esteem, poor relationships, reluctance to seek treatment or an inability to treat themselves effectively, along with distorted character development.

One of the most significant protective factors against the development of psychopathology in adulthood was having a good connection with one's parents when they were younger. Similarly, when developing and maintaining connections with other people, one of the most significant considerations is one's capacity to forgive the transgressions of others and experience sentiments of connection and love for those relationships.

Even if they have an anxious or ambivalent attachment style, young people can still maintain their social engagement and be ready to tackle their worries even with this form of connection. A kid's level of expectation for an attachment figure is proportional to the degree of trust the child has in that person. The degree to which a kid feels confident in themselves determines the degree to which they will enjoy the experience of engaging with a certain adult. This relationship is directly proportional to the level of enjoyment the child obtains from the interaction. A sense of proximity, the development of links, and the revelation that the significant other of the person having the intimate contact is exceptionally well known to the person having the encounter are all components that make up an intimate experience.

One of the requirements for entering into a commitment is a strong desire to love and the capacity to maintain that love over a protracted period. This is an essential need that must be satisfied immediately. Love that is not accompanied by a strong sense of commitment in a romantic relationship is love that does not have any value. This kind of love does not exist in healthy romantic relationships. The sensation of eros, which may be likened to falling in love at first sight, piqued the attention of the researchers for a variety of different reasons. There is a chance that this love will also not last, but there is also a chance that it will if the people involved work hard to strengthen their emotional connection with one another with time.

REFERENCES

- Ainsworth, M. D. S., Blehar, M. C., Waters, E., & Wall, S. (1978). Patterns of attachment: A psychological study of the strange situation. Lawrence Erlbaum.

- Howe, D. (2011). *Attachment across the life course: a brief introduction*. Palgrave Macmillan.

- Levitan, H. (2022, July 13). *If You Were Told To Be Highly Independent As A Child, You May Have Fearful Attachment*. Women's Health

- Li, A. P., MS, & MBA. (2021, June 18). *Fearful Avoidant Attachment - Causes, Traits & How to Overcome*. Parenting for Brain. https://www.parentingfor brain.com/fearful-avoidant-attachment/

- Maestre-Lorén, F., Castillo-Garayoa, J. A., López-i-Martín, X., Sarquella-Geli, J., Andrés, A., &

Cifre, I. (2021). Psychological Distress in Erectile Dysfunction: The Moderating Role of Attachment. *Sexual Medicine*, *9*(5), 100436. https://doi.org/10.1016/j.esxm.2021.100436

- Pascuzzo, K., Moss, E., & Cyr, C. (2015). Attachment and Emotion Regulation Strategies in Predicting Adult Psychopathology. *SAGE Open*, *5*(3), 215824401560469. https://doi.org/10.1177/2158244015604695

- *The 5 Best Attachment Theory quizzes On the Internet*. (2020, March 27). Greatest. https://greatist.com/health/attachment-style-quizzes#3

- Wade, R. (2021, December 7). *12 Anxious Attachment Triggers: How to Recognise & Heal Them*. The Feminine Woman - Dating, Love & Relationship Advice for Women. https://www.thefemininewoman.com/anxious-attachment/

- (2022). Study.com. https://study.com/academy/practice/quiz-worksheet-fearful-avoidant-attachment.html

- Ainsworth MD, Bell S.M. (1970). Attachment, exploration, and separation: Illustrated by the behavior of one-year-olds in a strange situation. Child Dev.;

41(1):49-67. doi:10.2307/1127388

- Ainsworth, Mary S. (1979). "Infant–mother attachment." American Psychologist. 34 (10): 932–937. Doi:10.1037/0003-066X.34.10.932.

- Ainsworth, MD, Bell, SM. (1970). Attachment, exploration, and separation: Illustrated by one-year-olds' behavior in a strange situation. Child Development, 41(1), 49-67.

- *Anxious Attachment in Adults: Triggers & How to Heal.* (n.d.). Hers. Retrieved July 24, 2022, from https://www.forhers.com/blog/anxious-attachment-in-adults#:~:text=What%20Are%20the%20Triggers%20of

- Baldwin, M.W., & Fehr, B. (1995). On the instability of attachment style ratings. Personal Relationships, 2, 247-261.

- Barglow, P., Vaughn, B.E., & Molitor N. (1987). Effects of maternal absence due to employment on the quality of infant-mother attachment in a low-risk sample. Child Development, 945-54.

- Bartholomew K.(1990) Avoidance of intimacy: An attachment perspective. Journal of Social and Personal

Relationships. 7:147–178.

- Bartholomew, K., & Horowitz, L.M. (1991). Attachment Styles among Young Adults: A Test of a Four-Category Model. Journal of Personality and Social Psychology, 61(2), 226–244.

- Belsky, J., & Braungart, J.M. (1991). Are Insecure Avoidant Infants with Extensive Day Care Experience Less Stressed and More Independent in the Strange Situation? Child Development, 62, 3, 567-71.

- Benoit, D. (2004). Infant-parent Attachment: Definition, types, antecedents, measurement, and outcome. Pediatrics & Child Health, 9(8), 541-54.

- Berliner, L. (2002). Why do caregivers turn to 'attachment therapy, and what can we do is better? [Special Issue: Holding Therapy: Part 2.] APSAC Advisor, 14(4): 8-10.

- Bifulco, A., Harris, T., & Brown, G. W. (1992). Mourning or inadequate early care? Reexamining the relationship of maternal loss in childhood with adult depression and anxiety. Development and Psychopathology, 4(03), 433-449.

- Blackman, James A. (2005) Infant Development and

Mental Health in Early Intervention. Austin, TX: PRO-ED Incorporated

- Bowlby J. (2004). *Teorie dello Sviluppo Psicologico*.20. Pp 71-74.

- Bowlby J. New York: Basic Books; (1973). *Attachment and Loss: Separation, anxiety, and anger.*

- Bowlby J. (1969). Attachment and Loss: Vol I Attachment. New York: Basic Books.

- Bowlby J. (October 1982) Attachment and loss: Retrospect and prospect. American Journal of Orthopsychiatry.664-678. doi:10.1111/j.1939-0025.1982.tb01456.x

- Bowlby, J. (1951). Maternal care and mental health. World Health Organization Monograph.

- Bowlby, J. (1952). Maternal care and mental health. Journal of Consulting Psychology, 16(3), 232.

- Bowlby, J. (1969). *Attachment and Loss: Volume I. Attachment.* London: Hogarth Press.

- Bowlby, J. (1988). A Secure Base: Parent-Child Attachment and Healthy Human Development. Tavistock professional book. London: Routledge.

- Bowlby, J. (2012). A secure base: Clinical Applications of Attachment Theory. London: Routledge.

- Bowlby, J. (1982). Attachment and Loss: Volume 1 Attachment. 2nd Ed. New York: Basic Books.

- Bremner, J. Gavin, et al. (2004). The Blackwell Handbook of Infant Development. Oxford, U.K.: Blackwell Publishing,

- Brennan, K. A., & Shaver, P. R. (1995). Dimensions of adult attachment, affect regulation, and romantic relationship functioning. Personality and Social Psychology Bulletin, 21(3), 267–283.

- Brennan, K. A., Clark, C. L., & Shaver, P. R. (1998). Self-report measurement of adult attachment: An integrative overview. In J. A. Simpson & W. S. Rholes (Eds.), Attachment theory and close relationships (p. 46–76). The Guilford Press.

- Brown, D. P., & Elliott, D. S. (2016). Attachment disturbances in adults: Treatment for comprehensive repair. WW Norton & Co.

- Brown, D. P., Elliott, D. S. (2016). Attachment Disturbances in Adults: Treatment for Comprehensive Repair. New York: W.W. Norton.

- Buescher. (2021, July 30). *Avoidant Attachment Triggers - Tips and Guide*. Attachment Project. https://www.attachmentproject.com/blog/avoidant-attachment-triggers/

- Bylsma, W. H., Cozzarelli, C., & Sumer, N. (1997). Relation between adult attachment styles and global self-esteem. Basic and applied social psychology, 19(1), 1-16.

- Carlson, E. A., Sampson, M. C. & Sroufe, L. A. (2003). Implications of attachment theory and research for developmental-behavioral pediatrics. Journal of Developmental and Behavioral Pediatrics 24(5): 364-380.

- Carlson, Elizabeth A., Megan C. Sampson, and L. Alan Stroufe.(October 2003) "Implications of Attachment Theory and Research for Developmental-Behavioral Pediatrics." Journal of Developmental & Behavioral Pediatrics 24, no. 5: 364+.

- Caron, A., Lafontaine, M., Bureau, J., Levesque, C., and Johnson, S.M. (2012). Comparisons of Close Relationships: An Evaluation of Relationship Quality and Patterns of Attachment to Parents, Friends, and Romantic Partners in Young Adults. *Canadian Journal of Behavioural Science*, 44(4), 245-256.

- Cassidy, J., & Berlin, L. J. (1994). The insecure/ambivalent pattern of attachment: Theory and research. *Child Development,* 65(4), 971-991.

- Christensen, L. B., Johnson, B. R., & Turner, L. A. (2011). *Research Methods, Design, and Analysis* (11th Ed.).

- Conrad, R., Forstner, A. J., Chung, M. L., Mücke, M., Geiser, F., Schumacher, J., & Carnehl, F. (2021). Significance of anger suppression and preoccupied attachment in social anxiety disorder: a cross-sectional study. *BMC Psychiatry,* 21(1), 1-9.

- Draper P, Belsky J.(1990). Personality development from the evolutionary perspective. J Pers.; 58 (1):141-61. doi:10.1111/j.1467-6494.1990.tb00911.x

- Early Childhood Research Quarterly, 11, 207-218. Hock, E. (1980). Working and nonworking mothers and their infants: A comparative study of maternal caregiving characteristics and infant social behavior. Merrill-Palmer Quarterly: Journal of Developmental Psychology.

- Esposito G, Setoh P, Shinohara K, Bornstein MH.(2017). The development of Attachment: Integrating genes, brain, behavior, and environment. Behav Brain

Res.; 325:87–9.

- Farrell, J. (2010). *Forgiveness, Mood, and Attachment Style*. https://etd.ohiolink.edu/apexprod/rws_etd/send_file/send?accession=dayton1283953274&disposition=attachment

- Favez, N., & Tissot, H. (2019). Fearful-avoidant attachment: a specific impact on sexuality? *Journal of Sex & Marital Therapy*, 45(6), 510-523.

- *Fearful Avoidant Attachment - How it Develops in Childhood*. (2021, June 7). Attachment Project. https://www.attachmentproject.com/blog/fearful-avoidant-attachment-in-childhood/

- *Fearful-Avoidant Attachment: 13 Signs & Relationship Patterns*. (n.d.). Www.simplypsychology.org. Retrieved July 17, 2022, from https://www.simplypsychology.org/fearful-avoidant-attachment.html

- *Fearful-Avoidant Attachment: Definition & Treatment - Video & Lesson Transcript | Study.com*. (2020). Study.com. https://study.com/academy/lesson/fearful-avoidant-attachment-definition-treatment-quiz.html

- Finzi, R., Cohen, O., Sapir, Y., & Weizman, A. (2000). Attachment styles in maltreated children: A comparative study. *Child Psychiatry and Human Development, 31*(2), 113-128.

- *Forgiveness as a mediating variable between attachment style and adult love relationships Dayna Northart.* (n.d.). Retrieved July 25, 2022, from https://digscholarship.unco.edu/cgi/viewconte nt.cgi?article=1041&context=dissertations

- Fraley, R. C., & Roisman, G. I. (2019). The development of adult attachment styles: Four lessons. *Current opinion in psychology*, 25, 26-30.

- Fuertes J N, R. Grindell S, Kestenbaum M, Gorman B. (2017) Sex, Parent Attachment, Emotional Adjustment, and Risk-Taking Behaviors, *Int J High-Risk Behav Addict.*; 6(2):e36301. doi: 10.5812/ijhrba.36301.

- Guy-Evans, O. (2022). Understanding the Fearful Avoidant Attachment Style In Relationships. *Simply Psychology.* www.simplypsychology.org/fearful-avoid ant-attachment.html

- Hamarta, E., Engin Deniz, M., & Saltali, N. (2009). *Attachment Styles as a Predictor of Emotional Intelligence.* https://files.eric.ed.gov/fulltext/EJ837780.pdf

- Harlow HF. (1958). The nature of love. American Psychologist.;13(12):673-685. doi:10.1037/h0047884

- Hashworth, T., Reis, S., & Grenyer, B. F. (2021). Personal agency in borderline personality disorder: The impact of adult attachment style. *Frontiers in Psychology*, 12, 2224.

- Hazan C, Shaver P. (1987) Romantic love is conceptualized as an attachment process. Journal of Personality and Social Psychology.511-524. doi:10.1037/0022-3514.52.3.511

- Hazan C, Shaver P.(1987) Romantic love is conceptualized as an attachment process. J Pers Soc Psychol.;52 (3):511-24. doi:10.1037//0022-3514.52.3.511

- Hazan, C., & Shaver, P. (1987). Romantic love conceptualized as an attachment process. Journal of Personality and Social Psychology, 52(3), 511–524.

- Hesse, E. (2008). The Adult Attachment Interview: Protocol, analysis method, and empirical studies.

- Hirst, S. L., Hepper, E. G., & Tenenbaum, H. R. (2019). Attachment dimensions and forgiveness of others: A meta-analysis. *Journal of Social and Personal Relationships*, *36*(11-12), 3960–3985. https://doi.or

g/10.1177/0265407519841716

- Honig, A.S. (2002). Choosing childcare for young children. *Handbook of parenting*, 5:375-405 http://www.unifi.it/offertaformativa/allegati/upload ed_files/2010/200011/B000294/Wikipedia-Teorie% 20dello%20Sviluppo.PDF

- https://www.womenshealthmag.com/relationships/a 40383169/fearful-attachment-style/

- Kaur, S. (2019). Diagnostic complexities in an adolescent with disinhibited social engagement disorder (DSED).

- Kavlak O. YayınlanmışDoktora Tezi. İzmir: Ege Üniversitesi Sağlık Bilimleri Enstitüsü; (2004). Maternal Bağlanma Ölçeği'nin Türk Toplumuna Uyarlanması pp. 16–22. 9.

- Keller, H. (2018). Universality claim of attachment theory: Children's socioemotional development across cultures. PNAS, 115(45), 11414-11419.

- Kennedy, M., et al. (2017). Adult disinhibited social engagement in adoptees exposed to extreme institutional deprivation: Examination of its clinical status and functional impact.

- Klain, E. J. & White, A. R. (2013). Implementing trauma-informed practices in child welfare. Washington, DC: ABA Center on Children and the Law.

- Kozlowska K, Hanney L. (2002). The network perspective: an integration of attachment and family systems theories. Fam Process.; 41:285–312.

- Kroupina, M. G., et al. (2018). Identifying reactive attachment disorder (RAD) and disinhibited social engagement disorder (DSED) in a clinical sample of high-risk children.

- Lerner, Claire, et al. (2004). Bringing Up Baby: Three Steps to Making Good Decisions in Your Child's First Years. Washington, DC: Zero to Three Press,

- Levy KN, Blatt SJ, Shaver PR. (1998). Attachment styles and parental representations. Journal of Personality and Social Psychology.407-419. doi:10.1037/00 22-3514.74.2.407

- Lyons, T. H. (2007). Attachment theory and reactive attachment disorder: theoretical perspectives and treatment implications. Journal of Child and Adolescent Psychiatric Nursing, 20(1), 27-39. doi: 10.1111 /j.1744-6171.2007.00077.x

- Lyons-Ruth K. (1996). Attachment relationships among children with aggressive behavior problems: The role of disorganized early attachment patterns. J Consult Clin Psychol.; 64(1):64-73. doi:https:10.10 37/0022-006X.64.1.64

- Lyons-Ruth K. (1996). Attachment relationships among children with aggressive behavior problems: The role of disorganized early attachment patterns. Journal of Consulting and Clinical Psychology. 64-73. doi:10.1037/0022-006x.64.1.64

- Lyons-Ruth, K., et al. (2009). From infant attachment disorganization to adult dissociation: relational adaptations of traumatic experiences

- Mahler, M.S., Pine, F., & Bergman A. (2000). *The psychological birth of the human infant: Symbiosis and individuation.* Basic Books (AZ).

- Main, M., & Solomon, J. (1986). Discovery of an insecure-disorganized/disoriented attachment pattern. In T. B. Brazelton & M. W. Yogman (Eds.), *Affective development in infancy.* Ablex Publishing.

- Main, M., Kaplan, N., & Cassidy, J. (1985). Security in infancy, childhood and adulthood: A move to the level of representation. In I. Bretherton & E. Waters

(Eds.), Growing points of attachment theory and research. *Monographs of the Society for Research in Child Development,* 50(1-2), 66-104.

- Mandavia, A., et al. (2016). Exposure to childhood abuse and later substance use: indirect effects of emotion dysregulation and exposure to trauma.

- Mikulincer M. (1998) Adult attachment style and individual differences in functional versus dysfunctional experiences of anger. Journal of Personality and Social Psychology.513-524. doi:10.1037/0022-3514.74.2.5 13

- Mikulincer, M., Shaver, P.R. (2007). Attachment in Adulthood: Structure, Dynamics, and Change. Guilford Press.

- Pearson. Etaugh, C., Williams, B., & Carlson P. (1996). Changing attitudes toward daycare and maternal employment as portrayed in women's magazines: 1997-1990.

- Pehr Granqvist, L., et al. (2017). Disorganized attachment in infancy: A review of the phenomenon and its implications for clinicians and policy-makers.

- Psy.D, E. M. (2021, July 9). *Fearful Avoidant At-*

tachment in Adults - Top Rated Miami Psychologists. Top Rated Miami Psychologists & Therapists. https://www.envisionwellness.co/fearful-avoidant-attachment-in-adults/

- Rattani, S. A. (2012). Women's Descriptions of Good Life. Asian Review of Social Sciences, 1, 1, 21- 30 http://trp.org.in/arss_Jan_June_2012.pdf

- Reisz, S., Duschinsky, R., and Siegel, D.J. (2017). Disorganized attachment and defense: Exploring John Bowlby's unpublished reflections. Retrieved from https://www.tandfonline.com/doi/full/10.1080/14616734.2017.1380055

- Sagi, A., Koren, K. N., Gini, M., Ziv, Y., & Joels, T. (2002). Shedding further light on the effects of various types and quality of early child care on infant-mother attachment relationship: The Haifa study of early child care. *Child Development,* 73, 4, 1166-86.

- Salter, M.D., Ainsworth, M.C., Blehar, E.W., Wall, S.N. (2015). Patterns of Attachment: A Psychological Study of the Strange Situation. New York: Taylor & Francis.

- Schaffer HR, Emerson PE. (1964) The development of social attachments in infancy. Monogr Soc Res

Child Dev; 29:1-77. doi:10.2307/1165727

- Schwartz, P. (1983). Length of daycare attendance and attachment behavior in eighteen-month-old infants. Child Development, 1073-8.

- *Self-Regulation Strategies for Anxious Attachment Triggers*. (2021, July 23). Attachment Project. https://www.attachmentproject.com/blog/self-regulation-anxious-attachment-triggers/

- Shuster, C. (1993). Employed first-time mothers: A typology of maternal responses to integrating parenting and employment. Family relations, 13-20.

- Simard V, Moss E, Pascuzzo K.(March 15, 2011) Early maladaptive schemas and child and adult attachment: A 15-year longitudinal study. Psychology and Psychotherapy: Theory, Research, and Practice.349-366. doi:10.1111/j.2044-8341.2010.02009.x

- Simmons BL, Gooty J, Nelson DL, and Little L.M. (February 2009) Secure Attachment: implications for hope, trust, burnout, and performance. J Organiz Behav: 233-247. doi:10.1002/job.585

- Simpson JA, Steven Rholes W.(2017 Feb) Adult attachment, stress, and romantic relationships. *Curr*

Opin Psychol.; 13:19–24.

- Simpson, J. A. (1990). Influence of attachment styles on romantic relationships. *Journal Of Personality And Social Psychology*, 59(5), 971.

- Soysal AŞ, Bodur Ş, İşeri E, Şenol S. (2005) Attachment Process in Infancy: A Review. J Clin Psy;88

- Spitz, Rene A. (2005). First Year of Life: A Psychoanalytic Study of Normal and Deviant Behavior. Madison, CT: International Universities Press

- Susman-Stillman A, Kalkoske M, Egeland B, Waldman I.(1996) Infant temperament and maternal sensitivity as predictors of attachment security. Infant Behaviour and Development. 19:33-47.

- The Infant Mental Health Promotion Project and the Department of Psychiatry,(1998) The Hospital for Sick Children. A Simple Gift: Comforting Your Baby [video]. Toronto: The Hospital for Sick Children

- Thompson RA. (2002). Attachment theory and research. In: Lewis M, editor. Child and Adolescent Psychiatry. 3rd ed. Philadelphia: Lippincott Williams Wilkins. pp. 164–72.

- Understanding Our Style of Relating When Triggered. (2011, August 22). *PsychAlive.* https://www.psychalive.org/understanding-our-style-of-relating-when-triggered-by-diane-renz-lpc/

- Van Ijzendoorn MH. (1995). Adult attachment representations, parental responsiveness, and infant attachment: a meta-analysis of the predictive validity of the Adult Attachment Interview. Psychological Bulletin. 117:343-387.

- Vaughn, B. E., Gove, F.L., & Egeland, B. (1980). The relationship between out-of-home care and the quality of infant-mother attachment in an economically disadvantaged population. *Child Development* 12 03-14.

- Waters, E., Merrick, S., Treboux, D., Crowell, J., & Albersheim, L. (2000). Attachment security in infancy and early adulthood: A twenty-year longitudinal study. *Child Development* 71(3), 684-689.

- Waters, S. F., Virmani, E. A., Thompson, R. A., Meyer, S., Raikes, H. A., & Jochem, R. (2009). Emotion Regulation and Attachment: Unpacking Two Constructs and Their Association. *Journal of Psychopathology and Behavioral Assessment, 32*(1), 37–47. https://doi.org/10.1007/s10862-009-9163-z

- Williams, P. (2022, June 20). *5 Clear Signs You Have a Fearful-Avoidant Attachment Style*. The Conscious W a y . https://medium.com/the-conscious-sign s-you-have-a-fearful-avoidant-attachment-style-ca81b 404c048.